Vision
America

By Aubrey Malphurs

*Developing a Vision for Ministry
in the 21st Century*

*Planting Growing Churches
for the 21st Century*

*Pouring New Wine
into Old Wineskins*

VISION AMERICA

A STRATEGY FOR REACHING A NATION

Aubrey Malphurs

Foreword by Leighton Ford

Baker Books

A Division of Baker Book House Co
Grand Rapids, Michigan 49516

© 1994 by Aubrey Malphurs

Published by Baker Books
a division of Baker Book House Company
P.O. Box 6287, Grand Rapids, MI 49516-6287

Printed in the United States of America

Library of Congress Cataloging-in-Publication Data

Malphurs, Aubrey.
    Vision America : a strategy for reaching a nation / Aubrey Malphurs ; foreword by Leighton Ford.
        p.   cm.
    Includes bibliographical references and index.
    ISBN 0-8010-6313-2
    1. Evangelistic work—United States. 2. United States—Moral conditions. 3. United States—Religion—1960- I. Title.
BV3790.M347   1994
269' .2'097309045—dc20   94-11200

To my friend and brother-in-law, Michael Womack, who carved out valuable time from his busy life and ministry to review and critique this manuscript. Also, to his special family who gave him permission and the time to do so—his wife, Claudia, and daughters, Katie and Emily.

89087

Contents

Foreword

*I*n the early 1950s I was a student at Wheaton College, preparing for a lifetime of ministry. Foreign missions were a big emphasis at Wheaton in those days, partly due to the influence of ex-GI's who had returned with a passion for missions from a world at war. Student missionary gatherings drew large crowds weekly. Our student body president, who was an outstanding basketball player, went to Asia for a career in missionary athletics. Some former graduates were speared to death by Indians they were seeking to evangelize in South America. These examples inspired many of us.

Forty years later my son, Kevin, having recently completed his education, is ministering to his own generation. Aubrey Malphurs's *Vision America* will be an important book for Kevin and his peers, for the United States itself is now a major part of the global mission field. In fact, the United States of America is today the largest mission field in the English-speaking world. It is estimated that there may be up to 250 million people in the United States who either are totally secular or have only a nostalgic memory of a religious past. Today there are more Christians per capita in Uganda than there are in the United States. Comparable figures may be cited for other parts of the world—with a higher percentage of Christians in Fiji than in any European country, and in Korea than in my native Canada.

When I began my work as an associate evangelist with Billy Graham, we could expect general community-wide support in most cities we visited. Schools would open assemblies. Radio stations might carry the meetings live. Businesses might contribute financially. We were like a high school football team playing on the "home field." Today in modern secular America, evangelism is like playing an "away game" at the opponent's field. The major social and cultural institutions are indifferent to, suspicious of, or outright hostile to the idea of evangelism.

Against the background of this major shift, Aubrey Malphurs has written *Vision America: A Strategy for Reaching a Nation*. As he assesses where we are, how we got there, and what we are called to do in our part of the global mission field, he is writing to those like my son and others who will be leading the churches to reach the nation in the decades ahead. Dr. Malphurs has brought together an important range of information. He covers many of the important phases in the development of secularism, generational change, the rival of "postmodernism," and the nature of change. At the same time he compellingly provides guidelines for ministry in a new era.

What are the requirements for leadership to meet the challenge? Three words stand out in this book: change, church, and character. Dr. Malphurs makes us face the reality of *change*, but in the face of change he emphasizes constancy, and faithfulness to God's call stated in the Scriptures and modeled in Jesus and the apostles. He emphasizes the *church*—both the planting of new churches and the renewing of traditional ones as God's agency to bring renewal in the midst of decay. And he insists on *character*—men and women, pastors, and lay people with leadership character that is visionary, trusted, and skilled.

In this emphasis he is entirely right. For some years in Leighton Ford Ministries I have been engaged in helping raise up the emerging young leaders for evangelism. We seek to help them lead more *like* Jesus in terms of character and to lead more *to* Jesus in terms of effectiveness. Increasingly, I find that young men and women are saying, "I need my vision sharpened. I need my character strengthened. I need to know the new ways in which God is working. Can you help me?" I believe that *Vision America* will help any leader who longs to serve God in this generation.

—Leighton Ford

Introduction

*B*obby works out regularly at a nearby world class health facility. He is tall, trim, and captained the volleyball team at UCLA in the 1970s. After graduation, he played briefly as a professional in Italy. Even at age thirty-six, he came within a fraction of making the Olympic team in Barcelona in the summer of 1992. In the process, he managed to finish a second bachelor's degree and a master's degree in sports medicine. In spite of all his education, he still is not sure of his niche in life. Presently, he lives in Dallas and is pursuing a medical degree at a major health-care facility with a national reputation.

In order to make ends meet, he keeps bar part-time during the late-night shift at a local upscale club frequented by the medical community. While he does not intend to keep bar for the rest of his life, he is proud of his abilities and the fact that with tips he is more than able to cover his expenses. In addition, he has met a number of prominent people with influence in the health-care profession. He suspects these contacts will prove valuable to him in the future.

Bobby's father divorced his mom shortly after he was born, and Bobby has always struggled in his relationships with women. He has been married once, but like so many Baby Boomer marriages, it ended in a divorce. Vowing not to make the same mistake again, he is living with Elaine, a Jewish girl, who is a promising new attorney in the city D.A.'s office. He is not sure if he loves Elaine. Regardless, they seem compatible and together earn enough money to cover school and to some extent experience the American Dream.

When he is not studying, Bobby and Elaine pursue an assortment of activities. They thoroughly enjoy attending the Dallas Mavericks' basketball games even though the season has been a bust. They have also participated in a variety of neighborhood projects from writing letters to save the whales to volunteering to tutor inner-city kids in a nearby project. Their remaining time is spent listening to the popular songs of the 1960s and 1970s—the Beatles, Bob Dylan, and even some Elvis.

While he was in grade school, Bobby's mom occasionally took him and his sister to a small, struggling church not far from where they lived in suburban Los Angeles. In spite of his erratic attendance, he managed to become involved in some of the weekend activities—especially volleyball. He did not understand what the preacher or the Sunday school teacher was saying. Most of the words were beyond his comprehension, and references to *sin* and *hell* accompanied by the preacher's ominous pounding on the pulpit frightened him. But he loved the hours he spent with the other boys and girls knocking a volleyball back and forth across a tattered net hanging over an aged asphalt court.

Bobby's involvement at the church slowed to a trickle during his last years at high school and ceased entirely after graduation. UCLA offered him a full scholarship to play volleyball. His mother had taught him well the importance of making good grades in order to get ahead in life. Athletics and academics left him with minimal time to attend church.

In fact, it was not even a consideration; the thought never crossed his mind. How can Christ's church reach Bobby and Elaine?

LaTonya lives on welfare along with her grandmother, eight siblings, and their five children in the inner city of Washington, D.C. At seventeen, LaTonya is a bright young lady of unusual ability according to her teachers, but she recently dropped out of school to have and care for her baby. She is not sure who the father is. Several boyfriends have come and gone, not to mention a rape, something that has become all too common for so many women in the projects. In fact, chances are good that her biological father is the father of her baby, though he only visits on occasion.

She has little encouragement to return to school. While it could provide a way out of the inner city, she, like her grandma, has given up hope. Her situation is desperate. Life for LaTonya has become a test of survival. Their small, one-room flat leaves much to be desired. It is impossible to keep it clean. Dirt collects easily and quickly in the many cracks and crevices as well as on abused second-hand furniture, crumbling plaster, and decaying linoleum floors. And when the people upstairs flush their commode, water drips down into her bathroom. Air conditioning is an unaffordable luxury in the summer, and the heating works only occasionally in the winter. The family survives on one meal a day consisting of canned foods provided by food stamps and a local gospel mission.

To venture out the front door is to face a world of crack cocaine, open prostitution, and cheap beer and wine. Drugs are simply a way of life in her community—as urban–American as hot dogs and apple pie. On every corner stand glassy-eyed Crips and Bloods wearing dark sunglasses. The envy of the kids, they flash large bankrolls as they wheel and deal near their flashy Mercedes or shiny, chromed Cadillacs. Most of the girls in this blighted community prostitute themselves to earn sufficient money to survive the system. LaTonya has done everything in her power to resist this daily temptation but feels herself slowly drawn to it. While most suburban shopping centers feature Sears, Wal-Mart, and McDonald's, the projects display small, decaying shops, occasional bars, and multitudes of whiskey and wine merchants. This is LaTonya's world, and in order to survive, most her age have decided to embrace it. It is a nightmare, but is there anything else?

LaTonya's grandmother is very religious and claims she used to attend a holiness church before moving to the projects. Now the only thing resembling a church is a nearby rescue mission that is frequented mostly by street people and down-and-outers in search of a hot meal. LaTonya has heard of Jesus from her grandma but has no idea who he is or what he has done in spite of the fact that his dusty, faded picture hangs on their wall. They used to own a tattered Bible, but the last time someone broke into their flat, he took it along with a malfunctioning Sony Walkman and a faltering television set from Goodwill. Few religious groups venture into this complex; Black Muslims are attempting to reach the males with some success. How can Christ's church reach LaTonya and those like her?

Brian grew up by himself—a notorious latchkey kid. His dad left his mom shortly after Brian's thirteenth birthday, forcing the quick sale of their home and a move to an apartment closer to the local television network where Mom worked. His father consistently helped with the finances until he remarried, but after that the funds dried up, forcing Mom to work longer and later.

Brian, now twenty-three, was angry that Mom had even hinted that it was time for him to move out and find his own apartment. Living at home provided a stable base of operations while he dabbled at college and one part-time job after another. His college-educated mom could not understand his aimlessness in life as she attempted to climb the corporate ladder with her eye on the position of vice president of news programming. Brian graduated from public high school with low SAT scores but managed to get accepted at the local community college. Aspiring to be a programmer analyst, he took only computer courses, avoiding English, math, and history as much as possible. Often he overheard his dad, who had agreed to pay for his education, refer to him as a "dumb kid." That hurt, and the pain only worsened when his mom suggested that he get serious about school or drop out. The work world proved to be a constant game of hopscotch from one low-wage/low-benefit job to another. He worked as a pizza driver, Wal-Mart shelf-stocker, and a health-care trainer at the local Y. Most recently, he has located a job as a security officer with a data processing company. However, without a college degree the chances of any kind of a promotion are slim. He is currently looking for another job that could provide enough income should he be forced to live on his own.

Brian played high school basketball and displayed skills and abilities that attracted the attention of several local colleges. Though he was never offered a scholarship, he loves basketball and spends much of his time after work playing in a competitive men's league at the local Y. His weekends consist primarily of watching the cable sports network, reruns of "The Simpsons," and MTV. He practically inhales heavy metal and alternative rock. Among his favorites are Nirvana, the Red Hot Chili Peppers, and Guns 'N Roses. He does not care for rap and finds the lyrics of Ice-T much too radical.

As a loner, Brian has a few, carefully selected friends and dates only on occasion. He is an introvert who yearns for significant male companionship. However, most of his buddies have proved to be fair-weather friends lacking in integrity and authenticity. They, like him, represent a young-adult wasteland of academic nonperformance, political apathy, and job nomads who roam aimlessly in the service economy. Facing a world of recession, most feel neglected, shut out, and overwhelmingly pessimistic about their economic future and the long-term fate of the Baby Buster generation.

Brian's family was unchurched, but during his high school years Brian was exposed to several fellow students who studied the Bible and prayed together even though the public school forbade it. He admired their courage and convictions and attended some of their meetings. He was interested in spiritual things. They spoke of sin, repentance, salvation, and Christ's love, but he did not understand what they were talking about. They might as well have been speaking Chinese. Eventually, he lost interest when the school administration broke up the Bible study and the basketball season commenced. Later his interest was revived at the death of his grandfather, and he visited a church or two in the community. He found, however, that the services were geared to an older generation. He could not relate to the music, and the sermons were boring, too long, and not relevant to his world. Who will reach Brian and his generation?

Three young Americans, Bobby, LaTonya, and Brian, represent the future of the nation in the late 1990s and the early twenty-first century. The critical question is, who will reach them? While generally interested in spiritual truth, the large majority of Baby Boomers and Busters remain unchurched in this post-Christian era. The traditional churches attended mostly by Pre-Boomers have not and most likely will not reach them with the gospel of Christ. At the same time, certain events point to an emerging change in worldview that could lead to a fresh look at Christianity as intellectually defensible in a predominantly secular culture. New paradigm churches have the potential to interest these lost generations in spiritual matters. Can the church recover in time to fan the embers of change?

The American church can bridge the current impasse. It must rethink its mission, however, and develop a fresh vision and a new strategy for targeting lost America if it desires to have any influence on the twenty-first century. In fact, this is the idea behind the words *Reaching a Nation* in the subtitle of this book. I do not mean to imply that America was founded a "Christian nation" and that the appeal of this book is for a return to our Christian heritage.[1] This is not likely to happen. Instead, the idea is for the churches to exert a significant influence and have a major impact on the American culture. While many still remain unaware of the existing problems, others are looking for counsel and direction in their attempts to reach out to modern Americans. I have written *Vision America: A Strategy for Reaching a Nation* to aid denominational leaders, church leaders, pastors, church boards, and laypeople in accomplishing this purpose.

The book consists of two major parts. The first is entitled "Waking Up the Church" and seeks to alert the nation's churches to the stranglehold of secularism on post-Christian American society as it impacts them and the culture. The first chapter traces the rise of secularism in Europe and its impact on American society and the three generations of the twentieth century. The second chapter shows the spiritually deadening impact of American secularism on the American church. Chapter 3 sheds a ray of hope on the situation based on Matthew 16:18 and an emerging shift in worldview that is taking place in western civilization, which may be more favorable toward some aspects of Christianity.

The second part, entitled "Reaching Out to the Nation" presents a vision and strategy for influencing America toward Christianity in the twenty-first century. The fourth chapter defines *vision*, while the fifth presents the Savior's predetermined vision for his church.

The last three chapters formulate a strategy for reaching America. Chapter 6 emphasizes the vital role of church planting to the future of the American church. Chapter 7 focuses on renewing the declining traditional churches, and the last chapter calls for a revision of theological education that must begin to prepare leaders for ministry in the twenty-first century.

Part 1

Waking Up the Church

What would happen if you invited Bobby, LaTonya, or Brian to your church? Most likely, they are interested in spiritual matters but not in your church or any other organized religion. Paradigm changes are beginning to take place in America that signal the potential for a more fertile climate for Christianity in the twenty-first century. The problem is that the average American church that loves the Savior appears to be sleeping through this change. The typical church has become aware that something is wrong in its ministry because attendance is down and the average age of many members is approaching the midcentury mark. Yet its response is to turn over and go back to sleep or to lay in bed with the covers pulled up over its head.

1

The State of American Society
Smothered under
the Blanket of Secularism

★ Are you aware of any situations within the last few years in which someone has filed a suit to ban any religious practices or education in a local public school, to limit or eliminate nativity scenes on public property, or to enact zoning laws to prohibit churches from meeting in private homes for any reason? How do you explain this?

★ What does the term *secularism* mean?

★ Have you ever heard the concept of worldview? What is a worldview, and which worldview dominates your life?

★ Are you a Pre-Boomer, Baby Boomer, or Baby Buster? What is your generation's attitude toward life in general and religion in particular?

William Pritchard is a tall, blue-eyed teenager whose heros are not those of the average teenager in the typical American high school of the 1990s. He dreams of becoming an English professor and teaching the works of Keats and Shelley, two well-known poets who vigorously supported the Enlightenment thinking of the French Revolution. Pritchard, who was born into the Lutheran faith but is searching for a different religious belief, has become well-known himself as of late in the Dallas–Fort Worth metroplex of Texas. He has filed a lawsuit to ban student-led prayers during school sporting events. He sued the Carroll Independent School District and won a temporary injunction in November 1992 to stop his classmates from praying during their high school's football pep rallies.

Kelly Shackelford, the southwest region coordinator for the Rutherford Institute, plans to file a lawsuit in federal court to reverse the injunction. He states, "This is a societal trend of intolerance to the beliefs of others. It's kind of 'in' now to say, 'How dare you discuss your religious beliefs in front of me?'"[1] Shackelford's comments point out the secular spirit that has come of age all across American soil in the latter half of the twentieth century.

Other trends of intolerance are evident. Many school boards have removed any form of religious education from the public schools; some have also prohibited the Gideons from distributing Bibles to public school children; courts prohibit prayer in public school classrooms and nativity scenes on public property; a town in Virginia outlawed the singing of religious songs (Christmas carols) on public property and went so far as to hold the carolers at bay with armed guards; government bodies have taken control from the churches for health and education programs as well as programs for the poor; some cities have enacted zoning laws that prohibit Christians from meeting in groups in their homes; and the list goes on.

In June of 1993 some rays of hope broke across the nation's horizon. In the *Dallas Morning News*, Steve McGonigle reported: "The U.S. Supreme Court, in separate rulings Monday, gave religious groups greater access to public school property and let stand a lower court decision permitting Texas students to conduct graduation prayers."[2] In essence, the justices ruled unanimously that school authorities must allow religious groups access to school facilities after hours if they do the same with nonreligious organizations. This decision established nationwide legal precedent that prohibits public school districts from barring access to their property based on the speech content of a group's activities.

In *A History of Christianity in the United States and Canada*, Mark Noll writes,

> Evaluation of the immediate past can be viewed as a balance between gains and losses. On the debit side, it is clear that standards of Christian culture have lost considerable power in the course of the twentieth century. . . . In the rest of Canada and in the United States, the Protestant mainstream that once dictated cultural values, provided standards for private and public morality, assumed primary responsibility for education, and powerfully shaped the media—that Protestantism is fragmented and culturally feeble. In short, institutions and values constructed with great sacrifice have been weakened and are now threatened with collapse.[3]

Noll concludes with a question and an answer: "Has North America become a religious wilderness once again? In considerable measure, the historical record suggests that it has."[4]

To this, the writers of *The Search for Christian America* add a sense of urgency: "We are in the midst of a cultural crisis. During the past two decades moral relativism has become much more visible in American public life. The constant celebration of self-indulgence that dominates the media and popular culture will certainly take its toll on whatever moral fabric holds society together. . . . Can a society based upon such moral relativism endure for long?"[5]

How did all this happen? How did the culture erode this way? The answer is threefold. The first is the erosion of a theistic worldview to one of deism and then to naturalism. Secularism[6] can be understood best in terms of the development of these three major worldviews of the West. The second is the rise of secularism in Europe, and the third is secularism's powerful influence on America and the three generations that have grown up on American soil in the twentieth century.

Worldview Defined

In his book, *The Universe Next Door,* James Sire gives the following definition of worldview: "A world view is a set of presuppositions (or assumptions) which we hold (consciously or subconsciously) about the basic makeup of our world."[7] We all have a worldview that is our essential intellectual framework or system of beliefs through which we correlate and make sense of all our experiences in this world. It serves as a pair of glasses through which we view reality. These presuppositions are necessary for thought to take place but by definition are unproven, and most operate on a subconscious level until someone challenges them with a different worldview.

According to Sire, a well-rounded worldview includes basic answers to at least five questions:[8]

1. What is real, or what is ultimate reality? (What is the nature and character of God and the universe?)[9]
2. Who are human beings? (What is the nature and character of humans?)
3. What happens to people at death?
4. What is the basis for morality and ethics?
5. What is the meaning of human history?[10]

Western Worldviews

In the Western world, two worldviews (theism and naturalism) are clearly dominant with a third (deism) acting as a transitional hinge between them.[11]

Theism

From the early Middle Ages up to the end of the seventeenth century, the foundational and most enduring worldview was theism. It is basically a biblical worldview. In response to the first question (What is real?), theism believes in an infinite, personal, triune God who created from nothing a universe with order and purpose and who is constantly involved in its ongoing operation (see Gen. 1:1; Col. 1:16–17). Next, it holds that human beings were created in the image of God with personality and dignity as male and female and were placed in charge of the earth (see Gen. 1:26–27). Third, people will die physically (see Heb. 9:27) but live eternally in heaven or hell as based on the acceptance or rejection of Jesus Christ as Savior (see John 3:16). Fourth, the basis for morality and ethics is a just and holy God who has given us absolute, moral standards for life as found in the Scriptures (see 2 Tim. 3:16). Finally, human history is best understood as linear, consisting of a meaningful sequence of events under the control of God and ultimately for his purposes (see Acts 2:23; 4:27–28).

Deism

In the late seventeenth and eighteenth centuries, deism served primarily in England and France as a transitional worldview bridging the chasm between theism and naturalism. Deism was short-lived as a dominant worldview, but it was in deism that naturalism found some of its roots.

While not all deists were in agreement, certain tenets were basic to this system. The deist response to what is real signals an alteration to the theistic view of God and the universe. Essentially, deists believe that there is a God who created the universe but left it to run on its own. Consequently, he is not personal, is not present with us, and, therefore, is not interested in (or in control of) the affairs of people. Deism held to a closed universe of cause and effect that operates much like a machine with humans as a reasoning and intelligent part of that machine/universe. We cannot know God through the Scriptures but only through the use of reason and the rational study of the world around us. Since most deists believe that God does not reveal himself through the Scriptures, ethics and morality are based on general revelation gained from nature.

Naturalism

Though a major worldview, deism did not prove to be stable. Sire writes: "Deism is the isthmus between two great continents—theism and naturalism. To get from the first to the second, deism is the natural route. Though perhaps without deism, naturalism would not come about so readily, deism is only a passing phase, almost an intellectual curiosity. Naturalism, on the other hand, is serious business."[12]

The reason naturalism is such serious business is because in many ways it is the complete opposite of theism, and it is the prevailing worldview in America at the end of the twentieth century. Sire writes of naturalism: "Born in the eighteenth century, it came of age in the nineteenth and grew to maturity in the twentieth."[13] Before Americans come to faith in Christ, most likely their worldview is naturalism. It dominates the universities and the public high schools and elementary schools across the nation, and it provides the framework for philosophical and scientific thought. Most important for this book, it undergirds American secularism.

What does naturalism believe is real? While theism believes in a personal, infinite God who is involved in the universe and deism believes in an impersonal God who abandoned it, naturalism takes the next step and believes that God never existed in the first place. Like deism, it holds that the universe operates on the basis of cause and effect within a closed system. However, because it does not believe in God as the architect, naturalism holds that the universe as matter has always existed. Human beings, like other objects in the universe, are matter, but they are unique among the evolving animal kingdom because they have developed abilities that animals do not have such as conceptual and verbal skills. When people die they simply cease to exist—life/matter is temporal, not eternal. Ethics and morality are based on the autonomy of human reason that denies the existence of absolutes. Every person is the captain of his or her soul and must decide for himself or herself what is right depending on the situation. Finally, history is linear and has no ultimate purpose.

To grasp the big picture of western thought and the development of secularism in Europe and America a basic understanding of these three major western worldviews is essential. The rest of this chapter will trace the development of secularism from Europe to America as driven and influenced by each worldview.

The Rise of Secularism in Europe

The Middle Ages

The study of the rise of secularism in Europe begins with the Middle Ages (A.D. 500–1400) and the growth and influence of the medieval church. During this period, Christianity gained broad public acceptance in the West and became closely tied to the state due, in part, to the influence of Augustine. At the same time, Aquinas's teaching on human will and intellect sowed the seeds for the later harvest of secularism.

How did the church gain public acceptance? Initially, the church flourished in spite of heavy persecution from the state. Around A.D. 313, Emperor Constantine ended the practice of persecuting Christians and made Christianity a legal religion and later (A.D. 381) the official religion of the Roman Empire. In the years to follow, Christianity experienced phenomenal growth and by A.D. 500 was firmly in place in western Europe. It held sway for over a thousand years with the result that some called the Middle Ages the "era of Christendom." Francis Schaeffer writes: "Europe was regarded as Christ's Kingdom—Christendom. Thus, Christian baptism was not only spiritually but socially and politically significant: It denoted entrance into society. Only a baptized person was a fully accepted member of European society."[14]

29

Augustine (A.D. 354–431) was one of the most powerful and influential people in the Middle Ages. Latourette writes: "No other Christian after Paul was to have so wide, deep, and prolonged an influence upon Christianity of Western Europe and those forms of the faith that stemmed from it as had Augustine."[15] In particular, Augustine's work *City of God* exerted a strong influence toward the amalgamation of church and state in an attempt to achieve a totally Christian society. While this gave Christianity and theism the home field advantage in terms of worldview, it also resulted in numerous abuses. The papacy became increasingly corrupt, and the clergy fattened themselves on the sale of relics and religious indulgences. The Inquisition was responsible for cruel and unusual punishment of religious dissent and created a repressive environment toward the scientific community as illustrated by its harsh treatment of Galileo. These abuses served to fuel the reforms of the Reformation and the strong move toward secularism in the Renaissance and the Enlightenment.

While theism was the dominant worldview, some initial seeds of secularism were present in the church itself and in the thinking of people such as Aquinas (1225–1274). The church contributed to secularism by a gradual distortion of biblical truth. For example, the authority of the church gained precedence over the authority of Scripture, and salvation was earned through a combination of faith in Christ plus human merit.

How significant was Thomas Aquinas to the church and secularism? Latourette summarizes: "Aquinas, more than any one else of the four centuries between 950 and 1350, provided Christianity with a firm intellectual foundation."[16] However, he believed that the fall affected people only in part. Humans were partly, not totally depraved—the fall corrupted the will but not the mind. Therefore, humans could rely on their intellect as well as Scripture. This attempt to synthesize faith and reason is found in his *Summa Theologiae*. Francis Schaeffer reveals the implications of Aquinas's view: "This eventually resulted in people believing they could think out the answers to all the great questions, beginning only from themselves."[17] In time, people began to think and act independently of the Bible. They were becoming autonomous. Philosophers either mixed the teachings of revelation with the reasoning of non-Christian thought, or they ignored revelation and relied totally on human philosophy.

The Renaissance

As the Renaissance (1350–1650) emerged in southern Europe in the fourteenth century, people redirected the focus on God, which characterized the Medieval era, to a focus on themselves. By the end of the Renaissance, the autonomy of humans that emerged in the former era had come full circle. People, not God, are now the independent, autonomous center of their own universe.

> In a broader sense the Renaissance may be defined as that era of cultural reorientation in which men substituted a modern secular individualistic view of life for the medieval approach to life. . . . The medieval theocentric conception of the world, in which God was the measure of all things, gave way to an anthropocentric view of life, in which man became the measure of all things. Emphasis was placed on the glory of man instead of upon the glory of God. . . . Although the age clung to religion, it was only as a mere formality upon the holy days of the Church, and the tendency was to forget the claims of God upon the individual in daily life.[18]

For people of the Renaissance, the present life was what counted. Either heaven, hell, or the afterlife were rejected or they were unimportant. In effect, people did not need God because they were totally self-sufficient to solve their own problems. Latourette sees the implication of this for our day: "This phase of humanistic strain was to contribute to the secularism which then and in later centuries was to be one of the most serious threats to Christianity."[19]

31

The Protestant Reformation

While the Renaissance emerged in southern Europe, another great movement, the Reformation (1517–1648) emerged in northern Europe. Like the Renaissance, it too was a reaction to the distortions of the Middle Ages. Both began with the same basic religious and secular problems but arrived at different conclusions. The Reformers concluded that the Bible is the final authority, not people or the church. Salvation is through faith in Christ alone—we cannot in any way merit eternal life. Contrary to Aquinas, both the will and the mind are fallen, and people are dependent on revelation not reason. Also, life is centered in the infinite, personal God, not in autonomous human beings.

With all these great accomplishments, how could the Reformation have aided in any way the spread of secularism? The answer is that it affected the influence of the church, which represented Christianity and theism. George Hunter observes that it did this in two important ways. First, it divided the church.[20] Cairns explains, "The Reformation meant the end of the control by a universal church. The corporate Roman Catholic Church was replaced by a series of national Protestant state churches in the lands where Protestantism was victorious."[21] Second, it turned the church's attention from managing society to managing itself in terms of personal renewal, reorganization, and its theology.[22] Again, Cairns explains, "a wave of religious energy vitalized the Church of Rome. This was the Counter Reformation or Catholic Reformation, which brought internal reform and resulted in the formulation of an official statement of doctrine."[23]

Ultimately, the Reformation and the Renaissance contributed to the so-called break up of Christendom and left a vacuum into which the already present forces of secularism quickly moved in the form of the Enlightenment.

The Enlightenment

Also known as the Age of Reason, the Enlightenment (1689–1789) followed both the Reformation and the Renaissance but was the logical extension of the latter. Francis Schaeffer summarizes: "It was thoroughly secular in its thinking. The humanistic elements which had risen during the Renaissance came to flood tide in the Enlightenment."[24] What were those elements? They include:

1. Human reason. At this time in western Europe, Enlightenment thinkers had totally abandoned divine revelation for human reason. This is why many called this period the Age of Reason. People were capable, by reason alone, of accomplishing anything they wanted.
2. A traditional morality resting on the foundation of reason. People could create a moral society based on reason. An enlightened world was no longer dependent on revelation, organized religion, or any one church.
3. A common, natural religion. While many religions exist, they are all part of a broader, natural religion. Therefore, truth can be found in all religions and no religion can claim exclusive rights to that truth.
4. The belief that education and knowledge are good and capable of delivering the inevitable progress that organized religion only talked about. While a particular church or religion may be helpful for the moment, ultimately, a person's faith is to rest in the advances of science and technology as forces for the common good.
5. People are intrinsically good. While they are capable of doing evil things, the blame must be placed on the environment, not the person. Consequently, a solution to the problems of humankind is to make this world a better place in which to live.
6. The universe is a closed, self-contained system. If there is a God, he has abandoned this world to operate on its

own. Therefore, miracles do not happen. If people want to improve themselves and this world, they will have to accomplish it on their own.[25]

Ultimately, these humanistic elements are only an outward expression of deism and naturalism that emerged as dominant worldviews at this time in western Europe. Again, deism arose first in the late seventeenth and eighteenth centuries, and naturalism followed in the eighteenth through the twentieth centuries. What is important to note is that, in general, deism attempted to maintain some kind of belief in God, whereas naturalism abandoned his existence all together.

The Influence of Secularism on America

For centuries European life and thought has strongly affected America. What cures in the intellectual wine cellars of Europe eventually is imported to North America. Therefore, it comes as no surprise that European secularism has found its way to American shores. A number of key Europeans, all products of Enlightenment thinking, have profoundly influenced modern times not only in western Europe but in America.[26] In particular, Europe produced men whom Martin Marty calls the major "god-killers": Darwin, Marx, Freud, and Nietzsche.[27]

Charles Darwin (1809–1882) had his greatest impact on American thought with his work in the area of biological science. He presented a natural, rational explanation for the origin of human beings through natural causes in a closed system. If there is no God, how do we explain humans and the universe? Essentially, Darwin postulated that biological life evolved from simpler life forms by a process called "the survival of the fittest." For the developing world of natural science, this was sufficient explanation. Who needs God as Creator? Others such as Thomas Huxley and Herbert Spencer popularized Darwin's foundational thinking and applied it to other areas such as the social sciences. Thus it began to spread and exert enormous influence on all of western thought. Karl Marx (1818–1883) argued that the central dynamic in the world is economic interest.[28] If people want to understand human behavior, they must understand economics. History is controlled by economic factors and, in time, those who are living off the misery of the majority will unite and emerge to create a new, fairer structure that includes all the people. Thus, Marx's thinking in the area of economics provided an alternative view of religion and the goal of history. Religion and the church are captive to economic interests. History culminates not in the glory of God in heaven and on earth but in a promised economic utopia for autonomous humans here on earth.

The thinking of Sigmund Freud (1856–1939) in the areas of psychology and psychiatry provided a naturalistic explanation for sin, religion, and a belief in God. How do we explain humankind's inherent belief in God, their need for religion, and the guilt they feel over sin if there is no God? Essentially, Freud's answer was to dismiss religion and all that it involves as a fantasy.[29] He argued that all neurotic behavior is founded in some way in sexual repression. Consequently, religion is the expression of some neurotic sexual fixation.[30] Salvation is found in sexual liberation.

Finally, Friedrich Nietzsche (1844–1900) was one of the first in the 1880s to reach the conclusion that, from the modern perspective, belief in God as a personal being is no longer tenable—God is dead. Religion, therefore, is merely the expression of personal weakness. Instead, each individual must learn to assert himself or herself and affirm and promote his or her own life, not God. Through wars and revolutions, in time, Europe will rid itself of the handicaps of the Judeo-Christian heritage, and a new ruling class will emerge that would become superman.[31] Paul Johnson comments:

> Among the advanced races, the decline and ultimately the collapse of the religious impulse would leave a huge vacuum. The

history of modern times is in great part the history of how that vacuum had been filled. Nietzsche rightly perceived that the most likely candidate would be what he called the "Will to Power," which offered a far more comprehensive and in the end more plausible explanation of human behavior than either Marx or Freud. In place of religious belief, there would be secular ideology. Those who had once filled the ranks of the totalitarian clergy would become totalitarian politicians. And, above all, the Will to Power would produce a new kind of Messiah, uninhibited by any religious sanctions whatever, and with an unappeasable appetite for controlling mankind.[32]

To some extent, Nietzsche was a prophet, as evidenced by the rise of such totalitarian politicians as Lenin, Marx, Mussolini, and Hitler. Hitler read Nietzsche and took him literally.

In light of the thought of the god-killers, Tom Oden argues that four cardinal motifs characterize modern times.[33]

1. Autonomous Individualism

In twentieth century America, people have come to view themselves as totally autonomous. Oden describes a human as "a self-sufficient, sovereign self."[34] Not only are people autonomous, they are individualists without a sense of community. A sense of connectedness is missing from their lives; each is totally disconnected from other people. This has surfaced in America in excessive individualism as modeled by the me-first-now generation, radical lesbian feminism, and so on.[35] Life has become personal, and people look out for themselves.

Autonomous individualism has provided the seedbed for both rationalism and privatization in America. Rationalism argues that a person can operate independently through the use of his or her mind. Knowledge is the key to advancement in this world, and people gain this knowledge on their own without help from God or any special revelation. Privatization cleaves the public and private spheres of a person's life. It makes a virtue out of saying, "My religion is personal; I prefer not to talk about it."

2. Narcissistic Hedonism

Narcissism is a love for or preoccupation with oneself. *Hedonism* is an excessive emphasis on the pursuit of personal pleasure. Narcissistic hedonism expresses itself in America in compulsive drug usage, sexual experimentation, and entertainment that is fixated on sex and violence. Its slogan is: "If it feels good do it!" And the results have been devastating: loneliness, divorce, and the substitution of sexual promiscuity for intimacy.[36]

3. Absolute Moral Relativism

All moral values are relative and subject to change according to the culture. Right and wrong depend on what the majority accept and are doing at a given moment in time. The common refrain is: "It must be all right because everybody is doing it." To believe something strongly is arrogance. Dogma is "out" while the pursuit of openness is "in." This relativism leads, in turn, to pluralism, which decides truth individually—whatever is true for you or for me is true. Oden notes the consequences of moral relativism in such areas as the condom dispute in the public schools and the hospital wards filled with crack babies.[37]

4. Reductive Naturalism

This teaches that only that which is verifiable is real. Thus, all forms of knowing are reduced and limited to laboratory experimentation, empirical observation, or quantitative analysis. The scientific method reigns superior as the method of gaining knowledge. All things can be explained by reducing them to their basic factors. For example, Oden notes that reductive naturalism reduces sex to mere orgasm, persons to bodies, psychology to stimuli, and so on.[38] The obvious difficulty is that reduction lessens in value and force. It brings into a lesser state and, thus, diminishes and impoverishes whatever it touches. Certainly, it leaves no room whatsoever for the awe and mystery of God. Faith and science cannot live side by side. Science rules, and faith is severely reduced if not jettisoned altogether.

The Generations of Americans

Three generations of Americans have grown up in the twentieth century under the creeping influence of secularism: Pre-Boomers, Baby Boomers, and Baby Busters.[39] The church of the 1990s and the early twenty-first century ministers primarily to them. For maximum effectiveness, it is critical that the church know and understand these generations.[40] Who are they, what has influenced and characterized them (see table 1), and what general effect has secularism had on each of them?

Table 1

Three Generations of Americans

	Pre-Boomers	Baby Boomers	Baby Busters
Formative Years	1901–1945 *GI Generation:* 1901–1924 *Silent Generation:* 1925–1945	1946–1964 *Early Boomers:* 1946–1957 *Later Boomers:* 1958–1964	1965–1983 *Older Busters:* 1965–1970 *Teen Busters:* 1971–1977 *Younger Busters:* 1978–1983
Formative Events and Influences	Rural Radio WWI, WWII, Korean War Depression Big bands Nuclear family Low tech Peace Campus quiet No gate	Urban-suburban TV Cold War Vietnam War Growing economy Rock 'n' roll Dual-income family High tech Urban riots Campus unrest Watergate	Urban-suburban Cable TV/VCR Persian Gulf War Busted economy Jazz, rap Dysfunctional family High tech Urban riots Campus quiet Contragate
General Characteristics	Single-career High birthrate Low divorce	Multicareer Low birthrate High divorce	Multicareer Low birthrate Higher divorce

Continued on next page

38

Table 1—*Continued*

General Characteristics	Low education	High education	Low education
	Respect authority	Challenge authority	Ignore authority
	Savers	Spenders	Savers
	Low health	High health	High health
	Private	Open	Cautious
	Early marriage	Late marriage	No marriage

Note: The idea for this chart, its general design, and some of its information is from Dr. Gary McIntosh, "What's in a Name?" *The McIntosh Church Growth Network* 3, no. 5 (May 1991): 1–2.

The Pre-Boomer Generation

Formative years. The *Pre-Boomer Generation* is the term coined to describe Americans born in the first half of the century from 1901 to 1945. They consist of two groups. The first is the GI Generation, born from 1901 to 1924, made up of notables from Walt Disney to George Bush.[41] The other is the Silent Generation, born from 1925 to 1945, touted as the leaderless Silent Generation because so far it is the first generation in American history never to have produced a president.[42]

Formative events and influences. Initially, rural America influenced the Pre-Boomers' values and lifestyle, however, this changed due to growing urbanization. This generation gained its information through the newspaper and radio. They faced major world conflicts such as World War I (1914–1918), World War II (1939–1945), and the Korean War (1950–1953) and experienced a severe depression at home (1930s). To solve their social problems, they looked to technology (the white-coated scientists) and big institutions. In fact, they were more enthusiastic about science and industry than faith.[43] Their music was the big band sound, and their families were nuclear, consisting of two children, a working dad, and a housewife mom.

The GI Generation was the "most powerful generational voting bloc in the history of global democracy. No generation in U.S. history—not even that of Jefferson and Madison—can match the GIs' lifetime record of success at getting, holding, and using political power."[44]

Generational characteristics. In terms of their work, Pre-Boomers were committed to sticking with one career with one organization for a lifetime. While their birthrate was high (especially in the 1940s), the divorce rate was low. People married young and stayed married. Up until the end of World War II, a college education was only for the elite. They held a deep respect for authority whether political, religious, or military. Emotionally, Pre-Boomers kept to themselves. Men, especially, believed that to express their fears and hurts was a sign of weakness and vulnerability. They were also a generation of savers; they believed in saving everything, especially their money. Finally, they paid less attention to their health, although they were not aware of all the hazards of alcohol and cigarettes.

Influence of secularism. While the American church was strong in the first half of the century, especially in the 1950s, the seeds of Enlightenment secularism had begun to sprout as early as the 1930s.

The influence of Enlightenment secularism on the Pre-Boomer Generation is reflected by their general outlook on life—it was pervaded by a deep, profound optimism. Arthur De Jong writes, "American optimism is the result of a number of factors, but surely one of them is the Enlightenment."[45]

De Jong notes several Enlightenment events that precipitated the enthusiasm. One was a sense of progress and hope for the political order as the result of the English and French Revolutions. Another was the great technological advances produced by the Industrial Revolution that made life easier for the average person.[46] World War II was believed to be the "war to end all wars." It was followed by a strong economic recovery. People believed that science and technology would make this a better world in which to live. The opening of the doors of colleges and universities to the returning GIs meant better jobs and an educated citizenry. Social and political progress was inevitable. A growing self-confidence left Americans with the sense that they controlled their destiny much as western Europe had believed during the Enlightenment.

The Baby Boomer Generation

Formative years. The term *Baby Boomer* is used to describe any of the seventy-six million Americans born between 1946 and 1964.[47] They consist of two groups. The first are the idealistic early Boomers born between 1946 and 1957. Singer Janis Joplin, chess-player Bobby Fischer, Marine officer Oliver North, and radical Jerry Rubin are just a few who represent the popular Dr. Spock cohort. They are what most people think of as Baby Boomers.[48] The second are the more realistic, late Boomers born between 1957 and 1964. They are best known as the less popular, pessimistic Me Generation.

Formative events and influences. Life for the Baby Boom Generation forms a stark contrast to the Pre-Boomer Generation. An urban and suburban lifestyle replaced a rural lifestyle. While not abandoning radio completely, television became the prime information source. Boomers grew up under the shadow of the Cold War but actually experienced only the tragedies of the Vietnam War. The economy in the 1960s was good with the result that the early Boomers were able to realize to a great extent the American Dream. However, it petered out in the 1970s, leaving the later Boomers with only a dream and not the economic fruits to accompany it. The big band sound was out and rock 'n' roll was in. The technology switched from low to high, and the nuclear family disintegrated as wives went to work.

Other significant events were the civil rights movement, urban riots, campus unrest, Watergate followed by the resignation of President Nixon, environmental and ecological

41

problems, and the nuclear threat illustrated by the Cuban missile crisis. Also, the early 1990s witnessed a change in the power base. With the election of Bill Clinton as president in 1992, the power has shifted to the Baby Boom Generation. A postelection editorial in the *Dallas Morning News* reported, "The Clinton-Gore victory represents the transfer of responsibility from one generation to the next. The much-touted 'Baby Boom' is now coming into its own."[49] Mary Ann Hogan wrote, "They'll be making decisions, setting policy, dominating the ideas, charting the course of the nation for at least the next 25 years."[50]

Generational characteristics. Two terms describe best the generational characteristics of the Baby Boomers in comparison to their earlier counterparts—*change* and *contrast.* With the Boomers, the industrial age changed to the information-technology age. The birthrate dropped considerably due to a fear of overpopulating the world. The divorce rate changed from low (one in four) to high (one in two) as Boomers were twice as likely to have experienced a divorce as Pre-Boomers.[51] The Boomers are the best-educated generation in history—twice as likely to attend college as their parents, and three times as likely as their grandparents.[52] To them it was important to question and challenge, not blindly accept authority regardless of the source. They were characterized as more open about personal struggles and life's disappointments than their predecessors (especially the men). Their obsession with staying young has promoted a fitness craze and left them highly health conscious. Chances are excellent that Baby Boomers will have two, three, even four careers, instead of just one—they are committed to their professions not their companies. Initially, in the 1960s their outlook on life was very optimistic—they were on the fringe of a golden era; they would change the world! However, that optimism turned to self-doubt in the 1970s.

Influence of secularism. The seeds of the Enlightenment that began to sprout and bloom in America in the 1930s continued to affect the 1960s. In general, American optimism continued to run high among the Baby Boomers at least through much of the 1960s, although a few weeds had sprung up.

The Enlightenment expressed itself through what Sydney Ahlstrom called "a growing commitment to a naturalism or secularism and corresponding doubts about the supernatural and the sacral."[53] Fueled by Charles Darwin's explanation of the origin of the universe and events such as the Scopes Monkey Trial in the 1920s, the biological sciences eventually replaced the biblical account of creation and the origin of humanity with the theory of evolution. Freud's naturalistic explanation for people's belief in God and the consequences of sin paved the way for various secular theories in psychiatry and psychology. Nietzsche's argument that, from the modern perspective, God is dead served to fuel the thought of the radical theologians and the death-of-God movement in the 1960s. Due to a misunderstanding of Einstein's theory of relativity, people embraced the belief that Americans live in a world where everything is relative—absolutes do not exist.

The Baby Bust Generation

Formative years. The *Baby Bust Generation* is the term that describes the sixty-eight million Americans born from 1965 to 1983.[54] They outnumber every other generation in America except the Baby Boomers. This generation consists of three groups. The first are the older Busters, born from 1965 to 1970. The second are the teen Busters, born from 1971 to 1977, and the third are the younger Busters, born between 1978 and 1983. Eminent Busters are people such as actors Michael J. Fox and Tom Cruise, athletes Michael Jordan and Mike Tyson, and performers Michael Jackson and Whitney Houston.

Formative events and influences. The Baby Bust Generation, like the Baby Boom, experienced an urban, suburban lifestyle. They were educated primarily by the pen of Dr. Seuss and television's "Sesame Street." Television remained the prime information source, but cable television to a large extent replaced public television in the form of MTV (hence the label "MTV Generation"), and the VCR added another dimension and greater control to television viewing. The major conflict was the popular Persian Gulf War with Iraq. Yet this generation witnessed the dismantling of the Berlin Wall and the end of the Cold War. For the Busters, the economy went bust. They, more than any others, have experienced the consequences of a stagnant economy and are the poorest of the generations—roughly one in five lives in poverty. While 1960s rock 'n' roll is still popular, they enjoy jazz and rap and dance to music that is hard-core and electronically blended with strains of "Sesame Street" and "HR Pufnstuf." The family continued to disintegrate. While single-parent families are common, perhaps "The Simpsons" television cartoon characters best represent a typical buster family—dysfunctional. Though a Baby Boomer is president and the Baby Boom is now in power, Baby Busters played a major part in Clinton's election. In fact, a Baby Buster will probably be president in 2020–2040, and they will constitute the majority of the Supreme Court in 2030–2050.[55]

Generational characteristics. The generational characteristics of the Baby Bust Generation are frightening. Like the Baby Boom, they have experienced a low birthrate. However, it is due largely to the fact that they are the most aborted generation in history—abortions rose 80 percent between 1973 and 1979,[56] and during the Buster years, one in three was aborted.[57] Also, many will face untimely deaths (twice as many teenagers were killed in 1988 as in 1965) and are the most likely to commit suicide in their teen years (they have set a record with five thousand suicides a year through the 1980s).[58] Fewer are benefiting from higher education, as their college completion rates fell from 58 percent for the class of 1972 to 37 percent for that of 1980.[59]

More Busters are remaining single (in 1990, 53 percent of the twenty- to twenty-nine-year-olds had not married), and some estimate that approximately 60 percent of Buster marriages will culminate in divorce.[60] Perhaps they are simply modeling their own early family experiences—40 percent of Busters come from broken homes.[61] Therefore, it comes as no surprise that the Baby Bust Generation is the most cynical, pessimistic of America's generations, blaming many of their problems on the Baby Boom Generation.

Influence of secularism. While the seeds of Enlightenment secularism have continued to bloom in the 1970s through the 1990s, many of those blooms have faded and share their soil with numerous weeds that have sprung up. The Enlightenment optimism that characterized the Pre-Boom Generation after World War II and the Baby Boom Generation in the 1950s and 1960s has faded to cynicism and pessimism in both the Baby Boom and Bust Generations in the 1970s to the present. Because they fail to see the depravity of Enlightenment-based secularism, American culture at the end of the twentieth century continues to push secularism to its logical extremes.

This has had a profound effect on America's values and morality. Americans now place a high premium on an individualism that has led to the pursuit of privatism and a preoccupation with one's own lifestyle. The fruits are veneer friendships of little substance and terminal marriages. One's faith or religion is personal and not to be talked about or shared with others. The important thing is doing one's own thing, whatever that may be, regardless of how it affects others.

De Jong argues that America's move to individualism has caused a profound shift in its basis of morality.[62] People turn inward to find their own basis of morality. The individual, not God, is autonomous, and everyone does what is right in his or her own eyes. Freedom is "in," absolutes are "out," and truth is relative. Allan Bloom writes that "almost every stu-

45

dent entering the university believes, or says he believes, that truth is relative. . . ."[63] The advances in science and technology, which the Enlightenment promised would ultimately liberate humankind, have failed to do so. Instead, Americans, especially young Americans, feel they are doomed parts of some elaborate social machine that is out of control.

Food for Thought

1. What are some definitions for *secularism*? Which do you like best?
2. What are some trends of intolerance that reflect a secular spirit in your community? Are they increasing or decreasing in occurrence? What are some possible future trends?
3. How important is a person's worldview? Why? How would you define it? What are some of the key questions of a well-rounded worldview? What are the three major worldviews, and which best describes yours? Which worldview most influences American society in the 1990s? How does this affect your worldview?
4. Mentally trace the spread of secularism through both Europe and America. Name some key people and specific events that contributed to the spread of secularism. What are some key elements of Enlightenment secularism? How has Enlightenment secularism influenced the Baby Boom and Baby Bust Generations?

2

The State of the American Church

Gasping for Breath

⭑ In your opinion, are the majority of churches in America growing, plateaued, or declining in both size and influence? On what do you base your answer? Do you have an explanation for this situation?

⭑ According to your observation, are the churches in your community growing, plateaued, or declining in size and influence? How about your church? How do you explain your church's growth, plateau, or decline?

⭑ In light of chapter 1, how has secularism affected the American church in general? Any specific examples? How has it affected the churches in your community and your church in particular?

The American church is immersed in its culture; whether good or bad, we cannot escape it. In an interview in *Leadership*, James Davison Hunter says, "American public culture, broadly speaking, is a river made up of two major tributaries. One stream is the biblical culture that largely originated from Puritan intellectual and devotional life."[1] This is the cultural heritage of many of today's churches. Hunter continues, "The source of the other stream is the European Enlightenment. This was an attempt, by people like Thomas Jefferson, to revive classical humanism."[2] This is the heritage of today's secularism. Unlike other countries, the trends of secularism in American culture coexist alongside the traditional religious practices of the American church. However, at the end of the twentieth century, one is gasping for breath.

The question is, What impact has secularism had on the American church in the latter half of the twentieth century? The answer is found in tracing the increasing influence of secularist thinking on the church through the various decades beginning in the 1950s to the present. While the seeds of secularist thought sprouted prior to the 1950s, they began to bloom in the 1950s and flower in the following decades.

The Church in the 1950s

Historical Context

After World War II, the United States entered a period of great affluence and self-confidence. A booming postwar economy created a large middle class who began a move from the cities to the suburbs. When the GIs came home, they were ready to settle down and establish families. Their memories of their childhood days in church and Sunday school with its stability and respectability beckoned to them and their families. As higher education opened up to them, they joined the burgeoning ranks of middle-class America and the mainline Protestant churches that were enclaves of the middle class.

State of the Church

The results of the veterans' extensive migration to the suburbs in search of the good life were twofold.

First, it brought about an unprecedented level of church building as the mainline denominations followed their population to the suburbs. Never before in American history had citizens been spending proportionately as much per year on church building and never before had a higher percentage of people been on church rolls. Attendance and monetary giving reached new highs. Second, as mainline Protestantism moved into the suburbs, theological differences became less important than they had been throughout history. Instead of focusing on their past theological identities, the mainline denominations downplayed their theological traditions and differences . . . to attract the suburbanites to their churches.[3]

Church planting was also important in the 1950s. Organizing new congregations was a major priority for the home mission boards of most denominations. "Millions of dollars were raised for new church building. A history of the first twenty-five years of the National Council of Churches reports that 3,198 new local churches were established from 1954 to 1957. A National Council of Churches projection for the future called for 2,000 new churches per year for the next twenty years."[4]

In general, the 1950s was a decade of religious revival, at least in terms of a culturally acceptable Christianity. Though some viewed this so-called revival as a superficial blend of religion and American democratic values, Christianity was "in." Church became the thing to do on Sundays. Religious leaders such as Billy Graham, Norman Vincent Peale, and Monsignor Fulton J. Sheen attracted great numbers of followers. Martin Marty writes that in 1940 church membership had grown to 49 percent. However, in 1950 it climbed to 57 percent, and by 1956 it had reached 62 percent. This crested at 63 to 64 percent with almost 50 percent of Americans claiming to attend church each week.[5]

Secular Influence

While Christianity appeared to prosper on the outside, the forces of secularism, though not as evident as in later decades, were at work on the inside. Church membership and attendance were up. However, Gallup indicates that religious and biblical knowledge were down. "Fewer than half in a 1950 survey could give the names of any of the first four books of the New Testament. And only 1 person in 3 could name all four of the gospels."[6] This leaves the impression that the impact of the religious revival in the 1950s was rather superficial—a mile long but only an inch deep.

Mainline Protestant Christianity in the 1950s could be characterized as a comfortable Christianity—a situation totally alien to the New Testament. While it appeared large and healthy on the outside, it was starving on the inside. The focus of far too many entering the nation's churches was on the good life, which being interpreted was a fixation on material concerns, narrow self-interests, and personal enrichment. And the technology was available to deliver the good life. For example, the arrival of television saw Sunday night church attendance steadily decline. Why get all dressed up to go to church when it was more fun to stay home and watch the "Colgate Comedy Hour" or the "Ed Sullivan Show"? Little interest was evident as well in the needs of people who were living in a hurting world without Christ, such as the various ethnic minorities trapped and entrenched in the nation's inner cities.

The Church in the 1960s

Historical Context

The vast changes in the 1950s are minor compared to those of the 1960s—a period of cataclysmic upheaval for the nation. Issues that had been developing for years came to a head in the sixties. America witnessed such events as the full emergence of the civil rights movement involving sit-ins, freedom rides, racial murders, and the passage of the Civil Rights Act in 1964; the assassinations of President

John Kennedy, Martin Luther King, Jr., Malcolm X, and Attorney General Robert Kennedy; unregulated urban and industrial growth creating difficult social conditions that erupted in the urban riots of the late 1960s; antiwar protests over the escalating war in Vietnam; the continuing Cold War with Russia including the construction of the Berlin Wall and the muffed Bay of Pigs invasion; the emergence of student protests at various universities against the military-industrial complex; the development of the atomic bomb and the subsequent arms race; the initiation of the women's liberation movement; and the rise of the youthful counterculture who pursued an alternative lifestyle of drugs and sex.

Martin Marty characterizes well the conflict of the late sixties: "The later 1960s saw Americans in conflict as seldom before: men versus women, young people versus their elders, leftists versus right-wingers, hawks versus doves, blacks versus whites, homosexuals versus straights, hippies versus squares, Eastern religionists versus conventional congregants, countercultural Aquarians against nostalgic upholders of the olden ways—these all conspired to show how diverse and restless, how unsettled Americans were."[7]

State of the Church

Rapid, cataclysmic change also had impact on the churches of the 1960s. The mainline Protestant clergy, laypersons, and Catholic sisters supported and became active in the civil rights movement and antiwar protests. Along with the new morality and Joseph Fletcher's situation ethics, a radical theology developed that included such proponents as Thomas Altizer, who proclaimed the death of God. The Supreme Court handed down a decision that prohibited organized prayer in the public schools. In 1962, the ecumenical movement was launched by the Consultation on Church Union, and the charismatic or neo-pentecostal

51

movement emerged initiating renewal in Catholic and mainline Protestant churches. Also, various Eastern religions gained in popularity.

The result was a decline in religious interest and involvement as expressed by drops in church membership and attendance. Gallup writes, "Church membership, attendance, and the trend on the importance people place on religion were declining, not only among Catholics but among Protestants (particularly among mainline church members) and Jews. Overall national attendance dropped from 49 percent in 1958 to 42 percent in 1969, with the decline most pronounced among young adults (21–29 years), down 15 points, and among Catholics, down 11 points between these two dates."[8]

As the chaotic sixties progressed, a growing number of Americans felt that religion and the church were losing their influence on the nation. "In 1968, 67 percent said religion was losing ground, five times the proportion who felt this way a decade earlier. Those who held this view generally cited one of four reasons: (1) Young people were losing interest in formal religion, finding it not 'relevant,' (2) the growing crime, immorality and violence; (3) materialistic distractions; and (4) the church was not playing its proper role in society—some said the church was not keeping up with the times, but an equal number said that it was too involved in current social and political issues."[9]

Secular Influence

It was during the tumultuous sixties that the emerging secularist worldview found its most fertile soil and quickly blossomed, greatly influencing the American mind and, in turn, the church. Chaotic change allowed secularists to openly challenge many traditionalist beliefs of the churches. Charles Darwin's explanation of the origin of the species had by now gained the allegiance of the scientific community and was the predominant view taught in many public schools and most colleges and universities. Advances in the natural sciences such as biology, astronomy, and geology challenged the popular, biblical world-view. The social sciences followed suit and imitated the empirical approaches of the natural sciences. By this time Einstein's theory of relativity was confused with relativism. While he believed passionately in moral absolutes, moral relativism became pandemic, much to his distress.[10] George Gallup adds,

> The view that religion was on the wane was held to an even greater extent among persons attending college. The key reasons given were that student life reflected the trend toward secularization in American life with its emphasis on material rather than spiritual values; religion was unable to meet the challenge of science and the intellect; religion as a whole was failing to solve contemporary moral, social and economic problems; and students associated religion with churchgoing and church participation, which they found unnecessary for the fulfillment of life.[11]

Wade Clark Roof indicates that virtually all of the Baby Boomers (95 percent) were raised in religious homes, which strongly reflects on the Pre-Boomer Generation and their attitude toward religion and church. However, he writes: "My survey of 1,400 baby boomers—selected by random polling in Ohio, California, Massachusetts and North Carolina—found that two-thirds dropped out of churches, synagogues, temples, mosques and other places of worship in their teens for two years or more."[12]

The Church in the 1970s

Historical Context

In the 1970s, the activism and cataclysmic upheaval of the 1960s gave way to disillusionment and cynicism. Gallup writes, "In fact, the early nineteen seventies might have marked one of the lowest points in national morale in history."[13]

Several events marked this decade such as the killings of the student protesters at Kent State University, where students learned that the establishment would shoot them if necessary to preserve the status quo. Though the Vietnam War finally ended, Watergate followed, which served only to further discredit the president and Congress, resulting in the resignation of President Nixon. People became concerned with the insurmountable environment and energy crises along with a severe economic recession and high levels of unemployment. Whereas the students of the sixties focused on the nation, its future, and national problems, the students of the seventies focused on themselves, their future, and personal problems. The older, radical Boomers who sought to change the world in the sixties to make it a better place in which to live gave way to the younger Boomers who became the Me Generation of the seventies.

State of the Church

The national mood of pessimism and cynicism affected the churches of the decade. Based on a survey of American Catholics in 1972, some sociologists questioned whether Catholicism would survive in the 1970s. The change in mood deeply affected Protestants. Beginning in the latter half of the 1960s and into the middle 1970s, the theologically liberal mainline Protestant churches began to experience decline in membership and attendance, especially among the youth and young adults. Martin Marty and fellow researchers attribute some of this to a shift in priorities away from church planting to support programs of social and economic justice. "What might be called a 'no-growth theology' took hold, and social involvement came to be set in sharp opposition to church extension, not only on economic but also on theological grounds."[14]

Other factors were a lower birthrate, population shifts away from areas where mainline churches were predominate, the pursuit of social issues that failed to attract the interest of American youth, and an increasing ecumenical spirit that devalued doctrine resulting in a loss of identity in an age that desperately sought a unique identity. However, a number of conservative churches, unlike their liberal counterparts, experienced some growth. These churches might respond to this with great pride; some might be tempted to pat themselves on the back for their evangelistic efforts. Jackson Carroll and his researchers indicate that this would be premature because this church growth is due primarily to the recirculation of the saints, not evangelism.

Thus it seems that conservative church growth, at least in the groups studied, comes primarily through a kind of circulation process, by which evangelicals move from one conservative church to another. To a lesser extent, new additions are the offspring of members reared in an evangelical culture. Proselyte-type converts are typically "switchers" from other nonevangelical or conservative denominations; however, this is the least important source of new members. Bibby and Brinkerhoff conclude that conservative churches do a better job of retaining those already familiar with evangelical culture—both transfers and children of members— than moderate and liberal churches do in retaining their members.[15]

Another explanation for growth among conservative churches is church planting. Conservative churches tend to plant more churches than mainline churches because of the latter's emphasis on social and economic programs.

In addition to the conservative churches, nontraditional and non-Christian religious groups that strongly appeal to the youth under thirty experienced growth in the sixties. Examples are the Jesus Movement, the cults as represented by the Unification Church led by Sun Myung Moon, and the popular Eastern religions.

Secular Influence

During the seventies, Enlightenment-based secularism continued to be a growing factor and a major influence on life in general and the church in particular. De Jong notes that during this decade "to many Americans, the mainline Protestant denominations had accommodated too much to an increasingly secular society."[16] A secular philosophy of life was predominant in the 1970s, especially among young people under thirty. America was clearly a pluralistic society with people from ever-broadening religious, cultural, and ethnic backgrounds. In fact, George Marsden believes that the pluralization of American society was the most important development that contributed to secularization.[17] The move was away from a so-called Christian nation tied closely to institutions and organizations to the privatization of religion. Religion became for the average American a personal matter. You should attend church only if it meets your needs. Americans were in search of personal freedom, autonomy, and the tolerance that so clearly characterized the Enlightenment mentality.

The Church in the 1980s

Historical Context

In contrast to the pessimism of the 1970s, the 1980s initially became America's era of confident, successful conservatism. This decade that seemed to be dominated by politics witnessed the election of conservative Ronald Reagan in 1980 over incumbent Jimmy Carter, Reagan's spectacular reelection in 1984, and the election of George Bush, Reagan's vice president, in 1988.

Fueling this surge of optimism was the performance of the economy. In a recession, the Reagan administration managed to cut the inflation rate in half, remarkably lowered unemployment, and created sixteen million new jobs. Even more significant was the fact that with the collapse of the Communist empire, America had won the Cold War. At the same time there were problems. One was the increasing size of the deficit. Under the Reagan administration the United States became the world's largest debtor nation. Also, people worked longer hours to maintain their lifestyle while amassing credit-card debt.

This same period was marked by multiple scandals. Some examples are Marilyn Harrell, known more popularly as "Robin HUD," who misappropriated federal funds; Charles Keating, who embezzled millions of dollars through his savings and loan operation; and Michael Milken of Wall Street's junk bond empire.

A question concerning the political climate of the eighties is, Has the American public become more conservative and shifted to the right? In "The Myth of America's Turn to the Right," Ferguson and Rogers argue that based on polling data the answer is, No. They write, "American public opinion has long been best described as both ideologically conservative and programmatically liberal."[18]

State of the Church

The state of the American church in the 1980s has proved to be a continuation of the 1970s. According to the *Yearbook of American and Canadian Churches 1989,* the mainline Protestant churches continued to see decline while conservative churches saw growth. The fact that conservative churches are growing should be encouraging. However, closer scrutiny indicates some striking problems. First, the term *conservative* could be misleading. For example, the Church of Jesus Christ of Latter-Day Saints, who have experienced phenomenal growth, are almost always included under the conservative banner. Second, the largest denomination reporting continued growth is the Southern

57

Baptists. Yet in *The Baptist Standard*, the Home Mission Board's news service, Mark Wingfield writes, "If Southern Baptist churches were a family of children getting medical check-ups, the doctor would declare 52 percent of them stunted and another 18 percent critically ill. The diagnosis: Most Southern Baptist churches are not growing. And many of the growing churches are living off infusions from their sickly sister churches through membership transfers. It is a phenomenon one expert has dubbed 'the circulation of the saints.'"[19]

Tex Sample writes, "In spite of all the publicity given to conservative and fundamentalist churches in recent years, they are not drawing any greater proportion of the population and are not reversing the trends in the United States."[20] Barna and McKay write, "Despite the millions of dollars spent on media ministry and evangelistic publishing, there has been no real growth in the size of the Christian population in the last five years."[21]

In 1988, Gallup conducted a poll of unchurched America. He reports, "In 1978, 41 percent of all American adults (18 or older) were unchurched; in 1988, that figure rose to 44 percent. . . . The percentage of unchurched adults, based on the Bureau of Labor and Statistics population estimate, projected to 61 million in 1978 and 78 million in 1988."[22] Others believe that 44 percent is too optimistic and set the percentage of unchurched much higher. In *How to Reach Secular People,* George Hunter sets the figure at around 60 percent.[23] In late 1993, a research paper, which is to appear in the *American Sociological Review*, sets the number at 75 to 80 percent. This paper questions Gallup's most recent 1991 survey indicating that 60 percent of America is unchurched and argues that when respondents are surveyed they tend to exaggerate and overstate their attendance. The paper's research is based on a count of people in the pews rather than a survey approach such as Gallup's.[24]

Along with the growth of unchurched America, many churches are dying. An article in *Ministry* states, "America is running out of churches. It's true. Studies show that, in the next few years, 100,000 churches will close their doors—an extraordinary figure when you realize there are only 350,000 churches existing in our country."[25] The problem with this figure is that according to the Glenmary Research Center there are 255,173 churches in America, not 350,000.[26] The most accurate figure probably lies somewhere between the two.

Finally, not only is the American church declining and the unchurched growing, but various cults and nonevangelical religions are filling the void. An example is the Mormon Church.

Today the Church of Jesus Christ of Latter-Day Saints, better known as the Mormon Church, is one of the world's richest and fastest-growing religious movements. Since World War II, its ranks have quadrupled to more than 8.3 million members worldwide. With 4.5 million U.S. members, Mormons already outnumber Presbyterians and Episcopalians combined. If current trends hold, by some estimates they will number 250 million worldwide by 2080 and surpass all but the Roman Catholic Church among Christian bodies. With such sustained growth, says Rodney Stark, professor of sociology and religions at the University of Washington, Mormonism "stands on the threshold of becoming the first major faith to appear on Earth since the prophet Muhammed rode out of the desert."[27]

The article indicates that unlike several decades ago, the average Mormon is not a third- or fourth-generation member but a first-generation convert. This is the result of an aggressive worldwide missionary effort that enlists more than 60 percent of all Mormons between the ages of eighteen and twenty-two in spreading the Mormon gospel door to door.[28]

Secular Influence

In the 1980s, most have become aware of the enormous influence that secularism exerts in American society. Essentially, it has gained control of the critical opinion-making centers such as the universities, the media, government agencies, the marketplace, and public education. At most public colleges and universities, the naturalist worldview has become accepted to the extent that it is a basic article of faith. Faculty and students who fail to embrace it are viewed as backward and closed-minded. Unlike the 1950s and even to some extent the 1960s, television and film rarely depict Christianity or Christians in a favorable light. In fact, its absence in the typical television family has become predictable—on the "Cosby Show," the Huxtable family never prays over its meals, and no mention is made of attending church or religious services. Government agencies are learning that they must operate on strictly secularist principles or face exacting scrutiny from the press. The marketplace most often does whatever is necessary to maximize profits. And public education has opted for what they claim is a values-free approach to education. Teachers may hand out condoms to students but are not allowed to lead them in prayer.

According to the First Amendment, it would be difficult to argue convincingly that in a pluralistic society public institutions such as those mentioned above should favor Christianity over all other religions and nonreligions. How would we Christians react if these institutions chose to favor Islam? However, at the same time, the judicial trend has been to read the First Amendment as forbidding not the *establishment* of religion but the *respecting* of religion. Secularists appear to be working toward the complete eradication of religion. Rarely, if ever, do they push for the equitable representation of all religious and nonreligious beliefs that are found in the community. This is a contradiction and reveals the true heart of much of current American secularism.

The Church in the 1990s

Historical Context

In contrast to the optimism of the early 1980s, the end of the 1980s and the early 1990s has witnessed a return to pessimism. The beginning of this decade was marked by the economy and politics. America faced a recession, and some economists even hinted at a depression. A mounting deficit due to excessive government spending, massive layoffs, and so on affected most Americans. Throughout the 1980s huge corporations such as General Motors, IBM, Sears, Wang, and the airline industry continued to do business as usual. Their failure to innovate and adapt to the consumer in a decade of megachange resulted in major losses of market share. Today's corporate landscape is littered with these dinosaurs that did not move fast enough. The marketplace began to cut back in order to survive. The result was massive layoffs of industry personnel—especially middle management. The economy became the number one issue on the American agenda.

In the public eye, the political arena turned from bad to worse. Political institutions such as Congress experienced a further loss of credibility due to worthless pork-barrel projects, check-kiting scams, alleged womanizing, and so on. Initially, the Bush administration scored a great victory in Operation Desert Storm but later lost the war at home due to the worsening economy.

In 1992, the American public decided to replace incumbent Bush with Bill Clinton. Americans voted their pocketbooks. With the Clinton administration, Americans witnessed the transfer of power from the Pre-Boomer to the Baby Boom Generation.

Another haunting problem directly related to the morality of the nation is the spread of the deadly AIDS virus. While more than forty million people worldwide have contracted AIDS, approximately one quarter of a million people in America have developed full-blown AIDS between 1981 and 1992. The enormity of the disease is evident in that it affects the entire community whether homosexual or heterosexual, infants as well as adults. Before the 1990s come to a close, everyone will know someone who is infected with or has died of AIDS.

State of the Church

The problems of the church in the 1980s carry over into the 1990s. The church as a whole continues to experience decline and the unchurched increase. Barna writes, "In the typical community, about 4 out of 10 adults attend church services during the weekend."[29] An article about former President Jimmy Carter and his church in the *Dallas Morning News* illustrates the growing unchurched phenomenon. Mr. Carter teaches Sunday school in a strongly traditional Southern Baptist Church. The article relates, "At least two weeks out of every month at Maranatha, Mr. Carter teaches the adult Sunday school class. 'I have a lot of people come to my class just to see the curious sight of a politician teaching the Bible,' he said. 'A good number of them when they leave tell me they've never been in a church before, and they had no knowledge of the Bible.'"[30]

Another issue is the growing multiethnic situation or the coloring of America. The complexion of the nation has changed. Most communities consist of some Hispanics, African-Americans, and Asians who speak English, as well as the Anglo community. The Census Bureau predicts, "The Hispanic population will increase from 24 million in 1992 to 81 million in 2050. The African-American population will grow from 32 million in 1992 to 62 million in 2050. The Asian population will rise from a projected 9 million in 1992 to 41 million in 2050."[31] The result is that the number of non-Hispanic whites will drop from 75 percent of the total population in 1992 to 53 percent in 2050, and by that year, nearly half the nation will be part of a racial or ethnic minority.[32] Churches seem unprepared to target and reach these multiethnic people who are a growing part of their communities across America.

Secular Influence

In the early 1990s, indications are that Enlightenment secularism is firmly entrenched and continues to deeply affect both the culture and the church. Wade Clark Roof has written *A Generation of Seekers*, which is the first large-scale study of Boomers' spiritual lives. In a preview of this book in *USA Weekend*, he writes that among those who have dropped out of church or synagogue, "less than one in four have returned to active participation in a place of worship. . . . 80% say you can be a good Christian without attending church."[33]

In the early 1970s, Francis Schaeffer donned the prophet's mantle and warned that America was quickly becoming a post-Christian nation. In the early 1990s, his prophecy is reality. Recently, the *National and International Religion Report* stated, "Haddon Robinson resigned the presidency of Denver Conservative Baptist Seminary. . . . Meanwhile, Denver's trustees concurred with Robinson's assessment that America has entered a post-Christian era, and from now on they plan to train future pastors as foreign missionaries assigned to an alien culture."[34]

The term *post-Christian* has become a common description for culture in America and the western world in the early 1990s. Os Guinness labels America a post-Christian culture in *The American Hour*.[35] George Hunter refers to the western world and America as post-Christian when he asks, "How can we reach secular people and communicate the faith in the post-Christendom mission fields of the western world?"[36]

In the early 1990s, the nation is a morally rudderless society with a fixation on material concerns, narrow self-interests, and hedonistic lifestyles. But will the new Clinton administration make any difference? The verdict is still out. So far the signals are mixed. On the one hand, two of his first acts as president were to push for the acceptance of homosexuals in the military and the reversal of the antiabortion agenda of the Bush era. On the other hand, he was the first President since Gerald Ford to refer specifically and warmly to Jesus Christ at the

National Prayer Breakfast. And while on vacation in 1993, he was deeply moved after reading Stephen L. Carter's *Culture of Disbelief*, which scrutinizes the political and legal approach that trivializes religious devotion in America. While the administrations of the past have been prochurch, the relationship appears to have soured. Church leaders who have looked to government to accomplish moral and spiritual objectives in shaping public policy will need to rethink their strategies.

Where is the church in all this? Though limited, the church in the 1990s still has some voice and presence in the national community. However, many in the church naively view secularism as some stranger knocking on the door in an attempt to enter the lives of Christians and the church from without. The fact is that it has always existed to some extent in the church, and the danger lies as much within as without the church. In *Vital Signs*, Barna and McKay write, "Rather than adhering to a Christian philosophy of life that is occasionally tarnished by lapses into infidelity, many Christians are profoundly secularized, and only occasionally do they respond to conditions and situations in a Christian manner. Recent research shows that many Christians are especially vulnerable to the worldly philosophies of materialism, humanism and hedonism."[37]

In evaluating the evangelical church, Michael Scott Horton writes:

As we gave away more territory, *we* secularized America. It was we who left a vacuum to be filled by alternative world views. Unbelief grows because the reasons for faith are either internally inadequate or because they are inadequately defended. It is easy to lay the responsibility on secular humanists, but it is not quite honest. And honesty is essential in an hour such as ours. We ourselves left the neighborhood of ideas and retreated into our own private ghetto, where evangelical religion has been aptly, though tragically, characterized as privately engaging, but socially irrelevant. Cox puts it this way: "Secularism . . . has relativized religious world views and thus rendered them innocuous. Religion has been privatized. . . . Secularization has accomplished what fire and chain could not: it has convinced the believer that he *could* be wrong, and persuaded the devotee that there are more important things than dying for the faith. The gods of traditional religions live on as private fetishes or the patrons of congenial groups, but they play no role whatever in the public life of the secular metropolis."[38]

In essence, the future looks grim.

Food for Thought

1. In which decade did the American church appear to be at its height? What caused this prosperity? Was it characterized by a deep spiritual commitment to the cause of Christ on the part of American churchgoers? What kind of impact, if any, did secularism have on the church at this time?
2. Which decade was characterized by chaotic change? What changed? How did this affect the American church? What impact did secularism have on the church at this time? Has the church ever recovered from this period?
3. Which churches are reporting growth in the 1980s and 1990s—mainline or conservative? How do you explain this?
4. What is the state of the church in the present decade? Identify some of the forces of secularism that are at work and how they are affecting the church.
5. What emotions did you experience as you read chapters 1 and 2? How do you feel at the end of chapter 2? Why?

3

Hope for the Nation
A Second-Half Comeback

★ Are you optimistic or pessimistic about the future of the church in America? Why?

★ Does the Bible comment on the longevity of Christ's church regardless of the country in which it is located? If so, where?

★ Is the administration in Washington prochurch or antichurch? What makes you think this?

★ Are you aware of any signs of revival currently taking place in America? If so, where?

With only twenty-eight minutes left in an AFC wild-card game at Buffalo's Rich Stadium in January 1993, the Houston Oilers held a commanding lead over the Buffalo Bills: 35–3. Frank Reich, a Christian and Buffalo's backup quarterback, replaced starter Jim Kelly when the latter seriously sprained his knee. Two other vital Buffalo players, running back Thurman Thomas and linebacker Cornelius Bennett, had gone to the sidelines with disabling injuries. Many Houston fans had already begun to celebrate as they joyfully watched their television sets or "channel surfed" while a few thousand fans in Buffalo began to sullenly file out of cold, windy Rich Stadium. And then it happened.

Precisely, almost machine-like, Buffalo, under the direction of Frank Reich, commenced a record-breaking second-half rally that knocked favored Houston out of the NFL playoffs. The final score: Buffalo shocked Houston 41–38.

At the dawn of the twenty-first century, the blanket of secularism is wrapped tightly around both the American culture and the church. History has recently proved that if any hope for a post-Christian country exists, it lies not in a prochurch administration in Washington (as some had hoped in the past) but in a growing interest in spiritual matters across America and in revival within the church.

In spite of the bleak, almost desperate situation describing the moral decline of the nation and the condition of the church in the 1990s, some evidence indicates that the twenty-first century could see a time of spiritual revival—a second-half comeback. The spiritual evidence is in Matthew 16:18, while the philosophical evidence is the condition of America as the nation transitions from a modern to a postmodern era.

Spiritual Evidence

If Enlightenment secularism continues to tighten its grip on the American church, the twenty-first century should view the church's funeral. However, the Savior indicates that this will not happen. He promises, "And I tell you that you are Peter, and on this rock I will build my church, and the gates of Hades will not overcome it" (Matt. 16:18). The vital signs may go flat, but the patient will survive. In fact, there are several indications that the vital signs will perk up.

Renewal Movements

Although evangelism is declining in the United States and Canada, the Holy Spirit as promised (see John 16:7–11) is working in the unchurched regions of America, among ethnic communities, and among previously neglected groups. Over the past few years, grassroots prayer movements have popped up in various locales. In the unchurched Pacific Northwest, Dr. Joseph Aldrich, president of Multnomah School of the Bible, has led as many as thirty-five hundred pastors and church leaders in four-day prayer summits involving worship, prayer, and confession of sin. Henry Blackaby, a prayer coordinator for the Southern Baptist Home Mission Board, has led significant groups of Southern Baptist pastors and laypeople in meetings of spiritual renewal. These meetings, called solemn assemblies, are devoted to prayer and the public confession of sins. Through his Concerts of Prayer ministry, David Bryant has led citywide interdenominational prayer gatherings in a number of American cities.

Even though North American inner cities have become hostile territory for Christianity, some churches across the nation have targeted ethnic communities for Christ. On the West Coast, Tom Wolf, the pastor of the Church on Brady, is reaching Hispanics and African-Americans in Los Angeles. Harvey Drake has ministered to hundreds of disadvantaged inner-city youths through various programs in Seattle. In the Midwest, Raleigh Washington, pastor of the Rock Church, is reaching both blacks and whites in urban Chicago. On the East Coast, Wellington Boone develops leaders among the black community in Richmond, Virginia, while Elward Ellis challenges African-American churches in Atlanta to reach many for Christ through active participation in world missions.

The Holy Spirit is also targeting the neglected Native American community for the gospel. The Christian Hope Indian Eskimo Fellowship (CHIEF) plans to reach every Native American in every tribe by the year 2000. Christians from certain tribes in Canada have targeted people in Idaho and North and South Dakota.[1]

Interest in Spiritual Matters

On an even broader scale, younger Americans are experiencing an increasing interest in spiritual things. George Gallup reports, "Perhaps the most prominent trend at present is the intense search on the part of Americans—particularly young persons—for spiritual moorings in life."[2] Gallup quotes an article from the *New York Times* religion editor Kenneth H. Briggs, who writes, "Spirituality is what people want . . . people are hungry for a direct relationship with God."[3] In the *Dallas Morning News* at Christmas 1992, Ann Melvin writes:

> We are all searching for a fundamental purpose for living, being, giving and getting. For we are living in a time of idealistic bankruptcy. Not only do we have no commonality of sense of a greater power than human existence, but it is politically incorrect to speak of such and down right rude to expect others to. But cut it any way you like, name it anything you wish, proscribe to it any rules, sex, politics, image or powers you want—we still want God. And so even if it isn't fashionable, we search for God. And call it Magic. Or Christmas Spirit. Or Something.[4]

Gallup's 1988 survey of unchurched America revealed "considerable potential" for a return to a more active church life. He writes, "The unchurched today are, by many measures, more religious than they were a decade ago, suggesting that they may be on the verge of becoming more active. For example: 44 percent say they have made a commitment to Christ, up from 38 percent a decade ago. 72 percent say they believe Jesus is God or the Son of God, up from 64 percent a decade ago."[5] The unchurched also hold to higher levels of traditional religious beliefs. Gallup writes, "63 percent believe the Bible is the literal or inspired word of God. 31 percent say religion is 'very important' in their lives, while 38 percent say it is 'fairly important.' 58

percent believe in life after death. 77 percent pray to God at least occasionally, and 41 percent do so at least once a day."[6] It would be a mistake to assume from this information that unchurched people understand such concepts as a "commitment to Christ" or that "Jesus is the Son of God." The remarkable thing is that secular Americans are even interested in these concepts.

Gallup believes that three key factors prompt this search. The first is a need for hope in difficult times that are characterized by intense drug use, high crime, and numerous social problems. Survey respondents convey a sense of desperation and ask, "Where else but to God does one turn in times like these?" The second is a great, gnawing loneliness more characteristic of Americans than other nationalities. This loneliness is causing Americans to seek the dependable, supportive fellowship that is found in small groups. The third is a growing disenchantment with modern lifestyles in the context of no rules and an "anything-goes philosophy in society."[7]

While Americans are interested in spiritual matters, they are not as interested in the typical American church. In *Moody Monthly*, Ken Sidey writes, "According to a survey by *People* magazine, Baby Boomers go to church an average of about six times per year. . . ."[8] Jack Sims writes that the average Baby Boomer attends church only 6.2 times per year— "less than half as often as average Americans over 40."[9] He explains:

> Most of the babyboomers I have interviewed describe their experience with church and religious media as boring, irrelevant or high-pressured. They say things like: "I don't like the music. It sounds old-fashioned and strange." "It's too one-sided politically." "They are always asking for money."
>
> Some young believers I meet as I travel around the country are trying to hang on to a religion programmed to the

tastes of the older generation. Others are hoping to find spiritual homes within parachurch organizations. But a growing number are deciding that the cultural pain of living inside traditional organizations is greater than the pain of pulling up their spiritual and emotional roots. Tom Stipe, the 33-year-old pastor of Colorado's second largest church says, "The church is the last standing barrier between our generation and Jesus."[10]

Leith Anderson, in *A Church for the 21st Century*, believes that a spiritual awakening is sweeping the world and is affecting America. But then he adds, "Spiritual interest, however, does not mean an interest in Christianity or the church. People want to experience the supernatural. They want to feel God. And they are looking everywhere."[11] For example, today's generation are disproportionately inclined to pursue meditation, special psychic powers, reincarnation, Zen Buddhism, astrology, and New Age thought.

The clear message is that as our world changes, the evangelical churches must change if they are to communicate the gospel of Jesus Christ to a spiritually thirsty generation. Churches cannot conduct business as usual but must constantly seek significant ways to convey the never-changing gospel in an ever-changing culture that demands relevance.

Increasing Government Opposition

Over the decades, the government has been a friend of the church. In fact, President Dwight Eisenhower, a newly converted Presbyterian, was viewed as the formulator of the faith on the highest level. He was considered a model for faith and life for many Americans in the 1950s. John F. Kennedy was a practicing Catholic, the first to ever be elected to the presidency. On numerous occasions, Miami newspapers reported seeing President Nixon taking long walks with Billy Graham on Miami Beach. Jimmy Carter taught Sunday school at Maranatha Baptist Church, a strongly traditional Southern Baptist congregation in Plains, Georgia. And George Bush was a practicing, traditional Episcopalian, who espoused traditional family values in line with the Christian view of the church. While there is no sign that the Clinton administration plans to persecute the church, a war is taking place in the area of values. President Bill Clinton and Vice President Al Gore, both professing Baptists, strongly advocate positions that cut against the grain of traditional values of American evangelicalism. In *Focus on the Family Magazine*, Rolf Zettersten warns, "Many conservative leaders, including Dr. Dobson, have expressed tremendous concern over the President's vowed intentions to remove all remaining restraints on abortion, to advance special rights for homosexuals, to place women in combat roles and to accommodate sexual promiscuity by adolescents. . . . The next four years seem bleak to all those who cherish such concepts as the sanctity of life, full-time motherhood, innocent childhood, parental authority and heterosexual marriages."[12]

Our first response might be to throw up our hands in frustration. But we must realize that these setbacks could illustrate well the principle in Romans 8:28: "And we know that in all things God works for the good of those who love him, who have been called according to his purpose." The history of the Christian church has repeatedly demonstrated that it grows and matures when it is at odds with the government. This was true of the early church in the first century, and it has proved true of the modern church in places such as Communist China and Russia in the twentieth century. When the church is a friend of the government, it becomes lazy and complacent. However, when the government opposes the church or goes so far as to openly persecute Christians, the church wakes up and takes seriously the call of Christ and a deeper commitment to him and Scripture. Professing and shallow Christians fall away, leaving those who are serious

73

about their faith to be the church as the Savior intended. Perhaps the actions of the Clinton administration will serve as an early wake-up call for the church in the late 1990s and the early twenty-first century.

Philosophical Evidence

Shortly after the election of Bill Clinton, an article in *Time* quoted George Bush, "We stand today at what I think most people would agree is a pivot point in history, at the end of one era and the beginning of another."[13] In a time of cultural megachange, many Americans sense that Bush is correct. Somehow and in some way the country is experiencing a shift from one era to another. It is a shift from the modern to the postmodern era.

The Modern Era

Chapter one describes western civilization in six movements. This chapter focuses on the modern period that Thomas Oden dates from the French Revolution in 1789 to the collapse of Marxism in 1989.[14]

Table 2

Western Civilization

Roman Period (753 B.C.–A.D. 500)	Reformation (1517–1648)
Middle Ages (500–1400)	Enlightenment (1689–1789)
Renaissance (1350–1650)	Modern Period (1789–1989)

Oden and a number of other thinkers observe that a fundamental shift in worldview is currently taking place in America. "Within the bounds of these two centuries, an ideological worldview has arisen and fallen, come and gone. This worldview is filled with the humanistic ethics and scientific values and idealistic hopes of the Enlightenment period. . . .

That worldview has been spiraling downward in a relentless disarray during the three decades from 1960 to 1990, the period of rapidly deteriorating modernity. The malaise is acute in the American setting and chronic in the Soviet setting."[15] James B. Miller writes, "Most observers of contemporary history acknowledge that western civilization is undergoing a fundamental shift in worldview. In addition, it is generally agreed that this shift has been spurred on by the discoveries and theoretical developments which have occurred in the natural sciences over the past 150 or so years."[16] Millard J. Erickson states:

> This modern world view has gradually, however, begun to erode. Slowly at first, and then with accelerating pace of late, this understanding of reality has revealed its inadequacies. The acceptance of the idea that the modern period is passing away has become increasingly widespread. The significance of this change should not be overlooked or minimized. We are not witnessing merely the displacement of one theory by another, or a conflict about some peripheral ideas. We are actually seeing a paradigm shift taking place before our eyes, as it were. The conceptions on the basis of which society has functioned for some time are changing.[17]

What happened? Diogenes Allen writes that the modern post-Christian world is passing away, and we are entering a postmodern era. The reason for this change is the crumbling of the pillars of western society erected during the Enlightenment.[18] Allen specifically mentions four pillars.

The first and most fundamental is that developments in cosmology, specifically the big bang theory and the movement away from a Newtonian cosmology, have seriously called into question the Enlightenment tenet that we live in a self-contained universe that has no room for God. The result according to Allen is that "all people are now in the position in which it is sensible to become a seeker. If people are sensible, they will earnestly want to know whether this universe is ultimate or not. There is therefore no need for Christians to continue to be defensive. . . . We have the opportunity and the task of turning people into seekers, as did Socrates, with confidence that if one seeks, one is likely to find."[19]

The second collapsing pillar is "the failure to find a basis for morality in society."[20] The Enlightenment mind believed that traditional morality and society could be based on reason rather than religion or revelation. It made no allowances for man's depravity (see Jer. 17:9; Rom. 3:23). The test tube of time has proved the formula false. Today, most have abandoned traditional morality for a "live and let live" or "live as you please" mentality. We have arrived not at a consensus of morality but at what the Book of Judges describes as a time when "everyone did as he saw fit" (Judg. 21:25).

The third Enlightenment pillar to crumble is the belief in inevitable progress.[21] Enlightenment thinkers believed that people are basically good and reasonable. Therefore, the answers to man's problems are found in education and social reform. Man is capable by reason alone of realizing a moral, secular society. Given enough time, science and education will bring about a new world void of such pressing problems as racism, crime, teen suicide, sexually transmitted diseases, and drug and alcohol abuse.

Reality paints another picture. In the 1990s, the universities remain at the very heart of Enlightenment thinking. Yet racism abounds on most campuses, and prejudice against minorities seems to be getting worse, not better. Crime in the cities and suburbs continues to rise, especially among the nation's youth. The number of homicides is staggering. Guns and knives have become so standard among teenagers that many schools have installed metal detectors. In light of an appalling dropout rate, popular athletes and Hollywood personalities encourage kids to remain in school. But far too many kids respond, "Why should I stay in school when I can get rich dealing drugs?" Second only to accidents, teen suicide has become a leading cause of death among the nation's teenagers. The spread of sexually transmitted diseases is approaching epidemic proportions, and AIDS continues to ravish the population while medical researchers look in vain for a vaccine and a cure. The war on drugs has proved a colossal failure. Substances such as marijuana and crack cocaine are becoming commonplace in elementary schools as well as junior and senior high schools. The final Enlightenment pillar to collapse is the assumption that knowledge is inherently good.[22] With the potential abuse of genetic engineering, the development of bigger and better weapons of war, and other abuses, science has proved its potential for evil as well as for good. Reality is that politicians and business people, not benevolent scientists, most often determine the use of our nation's powerful, developing science technology.

The Postmodern Era

While there is an increasing recognition that the modern world is eroding, philosophers, scientists, educators, and others express a willingness to look for answers in what many are calling the Postmodern Era. Western civilization is beginning to recognize that America is in the midst of a seventh movement (see table 3). Historian Paul Johnson traces the beginning of postmodernism to May 29, 1919. On that day, the Eddington expedition on the island of Principe off West Africa photographed a solar eclipse that confirmed Einstein's theory of relativity. This event has altered forever the Newtonian cosmology that has formed the framework for scientific thinking from the eighteenth-century Enlightenment up to the present.[23]

Scientists today have begun to abandon the paradigms of modern science based on Enlightenment Newtonian principles and are adopting a postmodern science paradigm. The former viewed the world as closed and unchanging, without

77

mystery. Everything could be explained.[24] The latter views the world as open and changing, with mystery. Some things cannot be explained—leaving room for God.

	Table 3
Western Civilization	
Roman Period (753 B.C.–A.D. 500)	Enlightenment (1689–1789)
Middle Ages (500–1400)	Modern Period (1789–1989)
Renaissance (1350–1650)	Postmodern Period (1919–present)
Reformation (1517–1648)	

Diogenes Allen correctly argues that in this emerging postmodern world Christianity has become intellectually relevant. "It is relevant to the fundamental questions, Why does the world exist? and, Why does it have its present order? It is relevant to the discussion of the foundations of morality and society, especially as regards the significance of human beings. The recognition that Christianity is relevant to our society, and relevant not only to the heart but to the mind as well, is a major change in our cultural situation. The transition is hardly complete, but this is the vista which a postmodern world reveals."[25]

Again, in *Christian Belief in a Postmodern World*, Allen writes, "In fact, in the reevaluation of the intellectual viability of Christianity which is undertaken in this book, we shall see that not only are the barriers to Christian belief erected by the modern mentality collapsing, but that philosophy and science, once used to undermine belief in God, are now seen in some respects as actually pointing toward God."[26]

Thomas Oden's observations of postmodernism are heartening. In an attempt to discern where this emerging movement is headed, he writes,

All we can be reasonably sure of is that it is not likely to be a rerun of modernity. . . . Above all, postmodern consciousness will be searching for the recovery of the family, for enduring marriages and good environments for the growth and nurture of children. Postmodernity whether East or West will be searching for a way back to the eternal verities that grounded society before the devastations of late modernity. The direction of postmodernity, in short, promises to be an organic approach to incremental change grounded in traditionally vested values.[27]

The significance of the fall of modernism and the Enlightenment mentality for the American church and Christianity are best demonstrated in the life of Thomas Oden. Oden, a former theological liberal and professor of theology at Drew University, describes his odyssey from theological liberalism to the Christian faith and evangelicalism in the following:

> In describing the trek from modernity to postmodernity, I am in part describing my own autobiographical journey. After spending at least half of my life as a defender of modernity, what has changed from the old "me" is the steady slow growth toward orthodoxy (consensual ancient classic Christianity), with its proximate continuity, catholicity and apostolicity. . . . My old liberal friends think that what is happening to me is just the usual result of ordinary psychogenetic development, which is a polite way of reminding me I am growing quite a bit older, which I am grateful not to have to deny.[28]

This is not to argue for a Great Awakening or another Protestant Reformation in America, although the limiting factor certainly is not God. James Davison Hunter writes, "A Third Great Awakening , or a Second Protestant Reformation as it has been called, with the same amount of influence as the First and Second Great Awakenings in America, or as the original Protestant Reformation, is a virtual sociological, not to mention legal, impossibility under the present conditions of modernity. . . . The traditions of secularism have become too deeply ingrained in American culture and institutional structure to permit anything but, at best, a large-scale, private-sphere renewal."[29] Yet, in terms of the church's current condition, a large-scale, private-sphere renewal or revival in America would compare to a cool, refreshing breeze on a hot summer's day in Texas.

As we arrive at the end of the twentieth century, the intellectual climate in postmodern America is changing. For the first time since the Enlightenment, intellectuals are open to investigating various approaches to and explanations of life—including Christianity. It is only a matter of time before this spreads throughout the intellectual community and filters down to the typical American man or woman on the street. The question is, Will the church respond in time to use this potential opportunity to reach out to America with the gospel? I believe that it can. But it is in desperate need of a fresh vision and a significant strategy if it is to realize this mission.

Food for Thought

1. Describe the emotions you experienced as you read this chapter. Were they different from those you felt while reading chapters 1 and 2? If so, why?
2. Are you optimistic concerning the future of the church in America? Why or why not?
3. What spiritual evidence can you cite that might indicate a potential for revival? Are you aware of any renewal movements that are taking place in your community? Do you sense that people, especially younger Americans, are interested in spiritual things?
4. What philosophical evidence indicates a potential for revival? Do you sense that America is at a pivotal point in its history—that it is at the end of one era and the beginning of another? Why or why not?
5. When did America's modern period end? What are some of the causes behind the close of the modern era in

America? What happened in Russia at this time? Do you see any connection between the end of this era and the collapse of the iron curtain?

6. What are some of the characteristics of the postmodern era? Are you aware of any other evidence that might indicate that people are more open than in the past to investigate spiritual truth? What is it?

Part 2

Reaching Out to the Nation

With the dawning of the twenty-first century, the potential exists for the church to reach out to a Bobby, a LaTonya, and a Brian. Amazingly, Scripture has already touched their lives in some way in their separate journeys through life—in spite of the church's decline. Just think of the impact a robust evangelical church might have on them and the many others like them.

How might the American church that has appeared so indifferent to them and their various life situations change and reach out to them? I am convinced that the church as a whole and most pastors want to do just that but are uncertain how to accomplish outreach in these dizzying times of megachange and decline.

The rest of this book focuses on a strategy for outreach. A well-crafted strategy is always preceded by a powerful, significant vision. The development of a national strategy begins with a clear vision because a unique strategy is needed to accomplish a particular vision, and a strategy without a vision is like a cart without a horse—it makes no sense. The following chapters will articulate the vision necessary for the church to reach out and a viable strategy for accomplishing that vision in America.

4

The Definition of a Vision
The "Vision Thing"

★ How important is a vision to effective leadership in the nation's capitol, the marketplace, and the church?
★ How would you define the term *vision*?
★ Name some leaders, Christian or non-Christian, who are/were clearly visionaries. What kind of impact did they have on their generation?
★ Does your church have a vision? If so, can you verbalize it? If not, what effect has this had on the church?

Those who aspire to leadership in a troubled America in the twenty-first century, whether in the nation's capitol or the marketplace, must have a vision. Former President George Bush learned this the hard way when he lost his bid for a second term in the Oval Office in 1992. The press heavily criticized him during his re-election campaign for not having a vision for a nation with a faltering economy. In response, he made some passing remarks about the "vision thing," evidencing that he did not understand the concept of vision nor its importance.

In 1993, IBM sought a new chief executive officer to replace John Akers and to lead it into the twenty-first century. Akers had presided over the spiraling decline of the world's biggest computer company. James Burke, head of IBM's CEO search committee, was quoted in *USA Today*: "What IBM needs now is a creative visionary at the expense of technological know-how, someone who knows how to get people excited about change."[1] Diana Kunde wrote in the *Dallas Morning News*, "Insider or outsider, the person who replaces John Akers as CEO of IBM Corp. must be a visionary leader."[2]

It is imperative that Christians who would lead a sluggish, declining American church into the twenty-first century have a significant, focused vision for their ministries. I would define a Christian leader as a godly person (character) who knows where he or she is going (vision) and has followers (influence). Thus, vision is one of three critical components of a leader's makeup. Christian leaders must be able to articulate what God has called them to do. Not to be able to do so is to invite ministry disaster. People cannot focus on fog! If your ministry aims at nothing, it will hit it every time.

We need look no further than the Bible to find leaders who modeled a clear ministry focus. Moses demonstrated his acute knowledge of God's direction for the people of Israel when he appeared before Pharaoh and demanded their release from bondage to the Egyptians (see Exod. 5–7). Joshua took the leadership baton from Moses and completed the vision by leading Israel into the Promised Land (see Josh. 1–4). Nehemiah demonstrated that he knew precisely where he was going when he presented his vision to the king (see Neh. 2:5). The Savior ministered for three-and-a-half years in Palestine in clear pursuit of his vision—to die for man's sins and thereby provide salvation for all who would believe. Paul planted churches in Palestine, Asia Minor, and other parts of the Mediterranean world because of his vision to birth churches to reach non-Jews (see Gal. 1:16).

Lyle Schaller illustrates the importance of vision in *The Seven-Day-a-Week Church*. In this work, he directs our attention to the disproportionately large number of rapidly growing churches that have emerged in America consisting of churchgoers born after World War II. In arguing the number one reason why these churches have become so large, he uses the word *vision* four times.

> The number-one reason is not location or favorable demographics or seven-day-a-week programming or a particular theological stance. The number-one factor . . . is transformational leadership by a *visionary* pastor who knows how to rally people in support of a cause. To be more specific, these transformational leaders are completely convinced that people's lives can be transformed by the power of the Gospel. That is the number-one distinctive characteristic of these senior ministers.
>
> In addition, these transformational leaders (1) can conceptualize a *vision* of a new tomorrow, (2) can articulate that *vision* so persuasively that people rally in support of it, and (3) know how to turn that *vision* into reality.[3]

This chapter focuses on the definition of *vision*. Any discussion of *vision* must be predicated on a clear definition of the term. Miscommunication is often the fruit of conversations in which people mistakenly assume they are defining and using terms in the same way. Thus, though this section may appear to nitpick, it is necessary for the sake of clearly expressing ideas and concepts that are vital to Christian ministry. First, we will discuss what a vision is not. Often in defining a term, it is helpful to clarify what it is not in order to understand better what it is. This involves a look at various terms that are related to *vision* ("vision relatives") but should not be equated with it. The rest of the chapter will present and explain what a vision is.

What a Vision Is Not

The appearance of the term *vision* is relatively recent in Christian leadership circles.[4] Consequently, several terms have been used synonymously with *vision* in its early stages of development. I refer to these terms as "vision relatives" because, like uncles, aunts, and cousins, they are related in various ways but are not the same.[5] The following will focus on six vision relatives that are confused with *vision* and may appear in a church's ministry document.

Purpose

One term is *purpose*. At first glance, the terms *vision* and *purpose* appear the same. However, the term *purpose*, when used in context with the church, must be distinguished from *vision* for theological reasons. *Purpose* concerns the church's raison d'etre. It answers the question, Why?—Why does the church exist? *Vision*, on the contrary, answers the question, What?—What is the church supposed to accomplish in terms of its ministry?

According to Scripture, the chief end of man is to glorify God. The purpose of Israel in the Old Testament was to glorify God (see Ps. 22:23; 50:15, Isa. 24:15). The Hebrew term here has the idea of giving glory or honor to someone who is deserving of respect, attention, and obedience. It reflects upon the reputation of an individual. In the New Testament, the church's purpose is to glorify God (see Rom. 15:6; 1 Cor. 6:20) so that others will glorify him in response (see Rom. 15:9; 2 Cor. 9:13). The New Testament term *glorify* means to honor and is translated that way in 1 Corinthians 6:20. Consequently, the people of God are responsible to value, honor, or enhance the reputation of God.

This will always be the purpose of the church. It is an eternal purpose that will never change in its essential content and will only vary slightly in terms of its form or how it is communicated (see table 4).

The healthy church is to act and minister in its community in such a way that God's reputation is enhanced. This is essential in a time when secularism is deeply entrenched in America and the church is heavily under its influence. God's reputation in any community is directly proportional to the reputation of the churches in that community. If the lost generations of the twenty-first century are going to experience Christ, the churches in their communities will need to act and minister in such a way that God does not have a bad reputation.

Mission

Another term is *mission*. The reason for this confusion is well-founded—both *vision* and *mission* answer the important *what* question—What is the church's ministry? The mission of the church is clearly Christ's Great Commission (see Matt. 28:19–20), and as such it is timeless (see table 4). This is the unchanging post-Easter commission that Christ has commanded his church to accomplish in the world. Obedience to it also results in accomplishing the eternal purpose of the church—glorifying God. So what is the difference between this and *vision*?

Table 4

Purpose	
	Eternal *(Timeless)*
Mission	
Vision	
	Eternal-Temporal *(Timeless-Timely)*
Philosophy	
Strategy	
Structure	Temporal *(Timely)*
Paradigm	

The mission of the church is more goal- or objective-oriented. It is a basic "nuts and bolts" statement of the church's mission as found in a planning document. Every church must have a plan that is clearly expressed in document form. As some wise sage once said, "To fail to plan is to plan to fail." It is essential that this plan be written out if others are to understand, own, and follow it.

The mission statement is the critical part of the plan. Ultimately, the plan begins with and is built on the mission statement. Once the mission statement is established, the rest of the plan such as the strategy, budget, and calendar flow from it. In general, the mission states unequivocally what the church hopes to accomplish. The strategy states how the church will accomplish the mission. The budget focuses on the resources needed to accomplish the mission, and the calendar relates the time frame for the same. The wording of the mission statement might be described as "plain vanilla." For planning purposes it is worded much like the rest of the planning document—in matter-of-fact style.

The vision may or may not be found in the planning document. It serves not as part of the planning process but as a vital part of the communication process. At the very heart of the vision statement is the mission statement. They are the same in essence, only they are worded differently and have different purposes. On the one hand, the mission statement asks, What is the church's mission? On the other, the vision statement asks, What does it look like? What do you see in your mind when you hear the Great Commission? What does it look like when it is paraded through your church's community? What do you see when you dream about your church two, five, or ten years from now? It is the mission statement fleshed out in the lives of your people and those living in the church's target area. When a pastor plans the direction of his church, he develops and uses a mission statement. When he communicates that mission to his congregation, he translates it into a vision statement using fresh, contemporary terms that create pictures in people's minds.

For example, the mission statement of Lakeview Community Church in Cedar Hill, Texas (a suburb of Dallas), is "to honor our Lord and Savior, Jesus Christ, by carrying out his command to make disciples of all nations (Matthew 28:18–20)." It is followed by a vision statement:

Specifically, we believe God has called us to focus on reaching those in Cedar Hill and the surrounding areas who do not regularly attend any church. . . . As a result, the Cedar Hill area will be different in ten to fifteen years, with the Christian influence being increasingly felt in homes, businesses, education, and politics. We further intend to multiply our world-wide ministry by planting churches, by preparing our people for leadership roles in vocational ministry and para-church groups, by sending out missionaries, and by becoming a resource center and model for Texas and the nation.

The vision statement will not change in essence because, like the mission statement, it is the Great Commission. Its form or how it is communicated should change periodically, however, to reflect change in the church's culture and community over the years (see table 4).

Philosophy of Ministry

Another vision relative that is used as a synonym and is frequently confused with *vision* is *philosophy of ministry*. This concept has emerged in the last few years and appears widely in periodicals, journals, and books on Christian ministry. It regularly punctuates the classroom discussions of seminary professors and the conversation of those interested and involved in leadership and ministry. However, my investigations reveal that people are using the concept in numerous different ways with different definitions.[6]

A philosophy of ministry is the church's core values. These values dictate the church's priorities and shape all its ministry decisions. The vision rises out of them and is constantly influenced by them. If one of the church's core values is that lost people matter to God, then it will be reflected in a vision statement that seeks to pursue and win lost people for the Savior.

Whereas the vision and mission answer the *what* question, the philosophy of ministry answers the second *why* question—Why do we do what we do? The purpose of the church also asks the *why* question, but it focuses on why the church exists, not why it does what it does. The former is eternal in content, whereas the latter could vary if the church should in time change some of its values (see table 4).

The importance of a congregation's philosophy of ministry is that it shapes the congregational culture. In *Getting Things Done*, Lyle Schaller writes, "The most important single element of any corporate, congregational, or denominational culture, however, is the value system. . . . The values of any organization control priorities, provide the foundation for formulating goals, and set the tone and direction for the organization."[7]

What does a philosophy of ministry look like? How many values make up the typical statement? I recently surveyed several philosophy of ministry statements that I have collected from various churches over the past few years. Most list approximately seven biblical core values, usually beginning with the most important ones first. The following are the seven core values taken from the philosophy of ministry statement of Lakeview Community Church:

> *A Commitment to Relevant Bible Exposition*—We believe that the Bible is God's inspired Word, the authoritative and trustworthy rule of faith and practice for Christians. The Bible is both timeless and timely, relevant to the common needs of all people at all times and to the specific problems of contemporary living. Therefore, we are committed to equipping Christians, through the preaching and teaching of God's Word, to follow Christ in every sphere of life.

A Commitment to Prayer—We believe that God desires his people to pray, and that he hears and answers prayer (Matt. 7:7–11; James 5:13–18). Therefore, the ministries and activities of this church will be characterized by a reliance on prayer in their conception, planning, and execution.

A Commitment to Lay Ministry—We believe that the primary responsibility of the pastor(s) and teachers in the local church is to "prepare God's people for works of service" (Eph. 4:12). Therefore, the ministry of Lakeview Community Church will be placed as much as possible in the hands of non-vocational workers. This will be accomplished through training opportunities and through practices which encourage lay initiation, leadership, responsibility, and authority in the various ministries of the church.

A Commitment to Small Groups—We are committed to small group ministry as one of the most effective means of building relationships, stimulating spiritual growth, and developing leaders.

An Appreciation for Creativity and Innovation—In today's rapidly changing world, forms and methods must be continually evaluated, and if necessary, altered to fit new conditions. While proven techniques would not be discarded at whim, we encourage creativity and innovation, flexibility and adaptability. We are more concerned with effectiveness in ministry than with adherence to tradition.

A Commitment to Excellence—We believe that the God of our salvation deserves the best we have to offer. The Lord himself is a God of excellence, as shown by the beauty of creation; further, he gave the best that he had, his only son, for us (Rom. 8:32). Paul exhorts servants, in whatever they do, to "work at it with all your heart, as working for the Lord, not for men" (Col. 3:23). Therefore, in the ministries and activities of Lakeview Community Church we will seek to maintain a high standard of excellence to the glory of God. This will be achieved when every person is exercising his or her God-given spiritual gift to the best of his or her ability (1 Cor. 12).

A Commitment to Growth—Although numerical growth is not necessarily a sign of God's blessing, and is not a sufficient goal in itself, we believe that God desires for us to reach as many people as possible with the life-changing message of Jesus Christ. Therefore, we will pursue methods and policies which will facilitate numerical growth without compromising in any way our integrity or our commitment to Biblical truth.

Strategy of Ministry

A fourth concept that is frequently confused with *vision* is *strategy*. While the church's vision answers the *what* question and the philosophy of ministry the *why* question, the strategy answers the *how* question. The church's strategy of ministry articulates how the church plans to accomplish its mission and vision. It is not eternal in essence and should change periodically as the church evaluates its ministry effectiveness and adjusts accordingly (see table 4).

Again, Lakeview Community Church provides us with an example. Following its mission statement, it communicates the following strategy:

In order to accomplish this, Lakeview Community Church will be an equipping center where every Christian can be developed to his or her full potential for ministry. This development will come through:

a. creative, inspiring worship;
b. teaching which is Biblical and relevant to life;
c. vital, supportive fellowship; and
d. opportunities for outreach into the community in service and evangelism.

In my collection of vision statements, I have noted that it is common for visionaries to include the strategy of ministry statement as a part of the vision or mission statement in the church's ministry document. For purposes of clarification and communication, I would suggest that leaders separate the strategy, placing it after the vision and/or mission statement. This has the clarifying effect of saying this is what we plan to do (our vision or mission) and here is how we plan to accomplish it (our strategy of ministry). The philosophy of ministry would follow, explaining why we are pursuing this vision.

Structure of Ministry

Some confuse *vision* with *structure*. The structure of the church relates to the organization and arrangement of the various parts of the ministry, including the infrastructure, that serve to flesh out the vision. It comes after the development of the vision and would be a part of the strategy statement because it aids in accomplishing the vision and helps answer the *how* question. It consists of large-group and small-group ministries, various programs, staff and lay leadership, counseling services, the pastoral care system, the communication network, and so on. Along with the church's strategy, it would be found in the planning document, is not essentially eternal, and adjusts periodically to accomplish maximum ministry effectiveness (see table 4).

Traditional churches have typically structured their programs around Sundays and Wednesdays. Sunday begins in the morning with a Sunday school program and a preaching service at 11:00 A.M. Another preaching service is featured in the evening. On Wednesday nights, a small portion of the congregation returns for a prayer meeting. The problem is that many churches have adopted this structure from other, older churches that developed this structure around their original vision. Over the years, the intangible vision has been lost, but the tangible structure has survived with the result that the proverbial cart now leads the horse.

A number of new churches have adopted an innovative approach called the Meta-Church concept, developed by Carl

George of The Charles E. Fuller Institute of Evangelism and Church Growth.[8] It is not simply another program for the church, rather it affects the very way we view church itself. It does, however, provide a structure that allows for change in the size of a growing church without a radical restructuring of the church or its vision.

Paradigm

Finally, a somewhat recent concept that risks confusion with *vision* (especially in the future) is *paradigm*. Thomas Kuhn, who popularized the term in *The Structure of Scientific Revolutions*, used it initially with reference to the work of scientists.[9] It is beginning to appear in literature on leadership, change, and the church. Essentially, a paradigm is a particular shared set of assumptions, beliefs, mindset, or viewpoint about reality or how things are.[10] Joel Barker adds: "A paradigm is a set of rules and regulations that: 1) defines boundaries; and 2) tells you what to do to be successful within those boundaries. (Success is measured by the problems you solve using these rules and regulations.)"[11]

Each church represents a paradigm. The church's paradigm is the particular assumptions, beliefs, or viewpoint about reality adopted and shared in common by the congregation. It includes not only the church's doctrinal beliefs, but what the congregation thinks about its music, proper apparel, style of preaching, evangelism, the way it collects the offering, who sits where, when they worship, what they do Sunday morning, and so on. According to Barker's definition, it is the church's set of rules that defines the church's boundaries and tells you what to do to be successful within those boundaries, in short—it's how we see and do things around here. As such, the church's paradigm serves as a pair of glasses through which the congregation views their world, and it affects what they see and do within that world.

While no one church has precisely the same paradigm, a number of churches share similar paradigms—they tend to view life through the same set of glasses. They may prefer traditional church music that focuses on the grand old hymns of the faith, or they may feel that to dress formally on Sunday morning honors God. These congregations with similar paradigms are often referred to as traditional churches. Other churches see life differently. They may prefer a different style of music and dress casually, believing that it does not matter to God how they dress. Today, these congregations are often called contemporary churches. Tomorrow, they will become the traditional churches, and new congregations with a new shared set of paradigms will be called contemporary churches.

Paradigms are tenacious—they die hard deaths. The tendency is for them to prevail over long periods of time. They may last for years, decades, centuries, even millennia. Currently, phenomena originating in late twentieth-century urban American churches are challenging the phenomena that originated in nineteenth-century rural American churches. For example, in the past, a congregation paid the parson to do the work of the ministry. After all, he was the one in the community with the most education. Today all that has changed, and more laypeople are investing their lives in ministry.

The problem is that no paradigm is able to handle all the phenomena that come its way. In time, when enough unhandled phenomena build up, often the result is a new paradigm. The 1980s and the 1990s are experiencing this reality. A number of old paradigms are collapsing under the weight of new phenomena, resulting in the development of new church paradigms.

Later in this book, I will use the terms *old* and *new paradigm churches* in referring to some of these paradigm changes. A growing number of new churches are beginning to view church and life through a different set of glasses.

Thus, what these new congregations think about their music, preaching, evangelism, and church in general is changing. For example, the preaching is shorter in length, and preachers have become more vulnerable—willing to disclose their own personal struggles in life. Also, many churches have begun to form lay-led small-group ministries to accomplish pastoral care rather than depending on pastoral visitation. In addition, the meeting times have changed from Sunday morning and evening plus Wednesday-night prayer meeting to Saturday night or Sunday morning only.

How does the concept of vision relate to that of a paradigm? A church's paradigm is much broader than its vision and, therefore, includes the vision among other important ingredients such as the mission statement, philosophy of ministry, strategy, and so forth. The vision, in turn, serves as a vehicle to communicate to some degree the church's paradigm. It serves to keep the congregation informed of how it views reality, its assumptions, and its expectations.

What a Vision Is

Vision, in terms of leadership and ministry, exists on both a personal and an organizational level. Personal ministry vision focuses directly on a leader's unique design that helps in determining and directing that leader's future ministry direction. It comes as the result of discovering his or her divine design from God (see Ps. 139:15–16; Isa. 49:1, 5; Jer. 1:5; Luke 1:15; 1 Cor. 12:18; Gal. 1:15). This unique design consists of spiritual gifts, natural talents, passion, temperament, leadership style, and so on.

The discovery of personal ministry vision not only helps in the mobilization of laypeople within the ministry, it assists leaders in determining their future place of ministry within the body of Christ.[12] When an individual discovers that he or she has the spiritual gift of leadership and natural gifts in leadership, that person soon realizes that the ministry vision involves leading an institution such as the church from the point position. People with different gifts are placed in other positions that call for the exercise of their specific abilities. The practice of far too many churches in the past has been to place people in ministry positions based solely on their availability, financial income, political power, or other reasons rather than God's design.

Organizational vision relates directly to the ministry of a particular Christian organization whether a church or parachurch. Once leaders have determined their personal ministry vision, they should seek to identify with a ministry that has an organizational vision that aligns itself most closely with their personal vision. I define institutional vision as a clear and challenging picture of the future of a ministry as its leadership believes it can and must be.[13] This definition consists of six key ingredients.

1. It Is Clear

A ministry cannot accomplish anything of spiritual significance without a clear vision. Often when passengers board an airplane, the captain positions himself at the door of the aircraft and welcomes each one on board. Suppose that one passenger asks jokingly, "What's our destination?" and the captain replies seriously, "Beats me! Where would you like to go?" Would you climb on board? A plane cannot leave the airport unless the captain and crew know where it is going. To begin with, the leadership team must understand the vision. If they cannot articulate the dream for themselves, then they are not qualified to lead a flock, and they should not be surprised when no one follows them.

Next, the people who make up the ministry must clearly comprehend where they are going. Even if the leadership has a clear vision in mind, people cannot possibly follow unless they, too, clearly understand and own the vision. Consequently, an important aspect of leadership is vision casting. Leaders must articulate the dream for their people or experience tremendous frustration.[14] Scripture provides several models of leaders who were vision casters.

A prime example of a clear vision caster is Nehemiah. He made it known to all that God's vision for the distressed remnant in Jerusalem was to "rebuild the wall of Jerusalem" (Neh. 2:17). This is a concrete version of a more abstract vision concerning the restoration of Israel to a place where they glorify God and bring praise from all people for his name.

Another example is Moses, who clearly caught God's vision for Israel and communicated it to approximately two million people. The vision was simple and precise: Through the leadership of Moses, God was about to liberate Israel from Egyptian bondage and take them into "a land flowing with milk and honey" (Exod. 3:8).

2. It Is Challenging

A good vision energizes and catalyzes people. God placed his church here on earth to accomplish more than survival. If the dream does not challenge people, there might as well be no vision. One sure test is whether or not the leaders of a ministry are challenged by the vision. Does it fuel their enthusiasm? If it does not move them, then it will not move those who follow them. Church boards often carve out a weekend from their busy schedules to get away and conduct church business. Although this is an excellent approach to accomplish much of the church's business, it is not enough time to adequately develop a good vision statement. The result is a premature product that excites no one, and the statement dies a quick death in a file buried in some church cabinet.

Actually, challenging visions are best articulated by the senior leader. Most churches and some pastors make the mistake of assigning the development of a vision to some committee in the name of the priesthood of the believer. Most often, this process results in a watered-down idea that is acceptable to all but challenging to none. It fires nobody's imagination. Taking the lead in developing an inspiring vision is the point pastor's essential act of leadership. Vision by consensus robs the pastor of this opportunity.

The risks that leaders will take when challenged by a significant vision are amazing. Nehemiah was strongly challenged by God's vision to restore and rebuild the walls of Jerusalem. Otherwise he would not have risked communicating the dream to a potentially hostile King Artaxerxes and requesting his help in accomplishing the vision—it could have cost him his life (see Neh. 2:1–8). God powerfully challenged Moses with a vision to lead his people, Israel, out of Egypt and into the Promised Land. Had he not done this, Moses would not have risked his life and stood up to powerful Pharaoh or resisted the armies of Egypt.

3. It Is a Mental Picture

Visionary leaders have the capacity to see in their heads what many cannot see with the naked eye. That is one of the qualifications to lead leaders. After the completion of Disney World someone remarked, "Isn't it too bad that Walt Disney didn't live to see this!" Mike Vance, creative director of Disney Studios, replied, "He did *see* it—that's why it's here."[15]

Another example of this kind of sight is illustrated in the 1989 movie *Field of Dreams*, a tribute to all who dare to dream dreams and see what others do not see. The story is about Iowa farmer Ray Kinsella (Kevin Costner), who is inspired by a voice, "if you build it, he will come," to pursue a dream he can see but hardly believe. The dream involves turning his Iowa cornfield into a baseball diamond where "Shoeless Joe" Jackson and others return to play baseball. The film cleverly and sometimes humorously contrasts those who can see—the visionaries such as Ray, his wife and daughter, and

101

his friend, Terence Mann (James Earl Jones)—with those who cannot see—in particular, Ray's brother-in-law, Mark (Timothy Busfield).

Vision is a "seeing" word. John R. W. Stott says that vision "is an act of seeing—an imaginative perception of things, combining insight and foresight. . . . We see what is—but do we see what could be?"[16] A good vision challenges the imagination and creates exciting pictures in people's minds of what could be. They begin to see things and dream great dreams for God.

Visionary leaders carry in their mental wallets a picture of what their future ministries look like. No doubt Nehemiah carried with him a mental picture of the rebuilt gates from the time God gave him the vision until the gates were in place. Most likely Moses led the people of God in the wilderness with an imaginative picture of the Promised Land abundantly flowing with milk and honey.

4. It Is the Future of the Ministry

The leader always articulates a significant vision in terms of the future. It is a preferred future. It is a mental picture of what tomorrow looks like. It is a view of all the exciting possibilities of a ministry's future. In doing this, God's leader, empowered by the Holy Spirit, determines God's future for the ministry.

A scholar who had studied for a Ph.D. at Cambridge University in England tells of a history professor who not only studied the past but mentally projected himself into that past because he preferred to live there. Visionary leaders think and move in the opposite direction. They not only think about the future, they spend some time living in the future. In doing so they play a significant role in determining their futures. By cultivating God's vision for the church, leaders have a vital part in inventing and influencing the future of their ministries. They know precisely the kind of ministry God wants and where they are going with that ministry, and they press on toward the accomplishment of their goals.

The other choice is to dwell in the past or the present and ignore the future. This is a passive, reactive kind of leadership that lets future events shape the ministry. These leaders spend much of their time reacting to what happens rather than making things happen. Instead of setting fires, they spend most of their ministry time putting out fires. It is most characteristic of maintenance churches that are paralyzed by their problems.

This does not mean that visionaries ignore the present or the past. They use the present as a platform to launch their ministries into the future. They accomplish this by pointing to the inadequacies of the present ministry situation and thus create dissatisfaction with the status quo. Then they cast the vision of a better tomorrow and rally people toward it. Visionaries learn from the past but do not live in the past. An example is the apostle Paul who wrote, "but one thing I do: forgetting what lies behind and reaching forward to what lies ahead, I press on toward the goal . . ." (Phil. 3:13–14 NASB).

5. It Can Be

A good vision has solid potential. It rests firmly on the bedrock of reality. While it often tests the limits of what is possible, a good vision remains within the realm of the feasible. Visionary leaders believe that they are involved in something big for God. They take seriously Paul's challenge in Ephesians 3:20 to ask (pray) and think big. They are convinced that God is about to do something special that is going to make a difference and plans to use them in the process. They experience a growing awareness of what the church will be like. It is simply a matter of time before what *can be* becomes what *is*.

Leaders who lead with this perspective exert a strong influence over their people. They exude the kind of confidence in what God is doing that begets high credibility. Nehemiah went about leading the Jerusalem remnant in this manner. Throughout the early chapters of the book, he speaks and acts as if the walls were already in place. The reader can sense his great confidence in such passages as Nehemiah 2:20, where he assures the people, "The God of heaven will give us success." When God makes his will known, then leaders must boldly step out like Nehemiah and lead with confidence based on "thus saith the Lord."

6. It Must Be

Former President Kennedy once said, "Some people see things the way they are and ask why; I see things the way they could be and ask why not." Visionary leaders not only believe the dream can be, they are convinced that it must be. They regularly ask, Why not? A critical sense of urgency claims their lives and pervades their ministry. It has the potential of keeping them awake at night. Several reasons confirm this conviction.

First, visionary leaders believe that God is the source of their dreams. They are convinced that they are servants of God who are on a mission for God. Nehemiah expressed a sense of this divine involvement when he said, "I did not tell anyone what my God was putting into my mind to do for Jerusalem" (Neh. 2:12 NASB).

Second, visionary leaders believe that God will use them in some way whether great or small to accomplish the vision. They desire involvement and see themselves in a position to impact their generation much as King David served God's purpose in his own generation (see Acts 13:36).

Third, visionary leaders understand that God's vision will benefit people. They care about people and are convinced that people will be better off because of their dreams. This includes such benefits as eternal life, spiritual renewal, the reconciliation of a relationship, and much more. Nehemiah identified with and revealed his heart for people when he said, "You see the bad situation we are in, that Jerusalem is desolate and its gates burned by fire. Come, let us rebuild the wall of Jerusalem that we may no longer be a reproach" (Neh. 2:17 NASB). This does not mean that visionaries never get discouraged. A classic example appears at the end of Paul's life as recorded in 2 Timothy 4:9–16. This is one of the most discouraging passages in Scripture. Yet the visionary rarely envisions defeat, as evidenced by Paul's response to his discouragement in verses 17–18.

Food for Thought

1. Why is vision so important to good leadership?
2. Do you have a personal ministry vision based on your God-given design? If so, what is it? If not, has a lack of one affected your ministry career? How?
3. What essentially is the difference between a church's vision and its purpose, mission, philosophy, strategy, and paradigm?
4. Does your ministry have an organizational vision? If so, what is it? If not, how has this affected the ministry?
5. If you have developed a vision for your church, is it clear and challenging? How do you know?

5

The Great Commission

What Business Are You In?

⋆ Is the concept of vision as developed in chapter 4 biblical or extrabiblical in origin?

⋆ Has God predetermined the same vision for every church, or does he leave it up to each church to determine its own vision?

⋆ What is the Great Commission, and where is it found in the Bible?

⋆ Is evangelism best accomplished through directly confronting people with the gospel? Is confrontation evangelism your style?

Management guru Peter Drucker writes that every business must ask and answer certain crucial questions to be successful. Perhaps the most important question is, What business are you in? If a business struggles to answer this question, it will not survive in our fiercely competitive marketplace. It is vital that church leaders regularly ask the same basic question, What business are you in? Or better, What is Christ's church supposed to accomplish in the world? Failure to ask and accurately answer this question means that many local churches will not survive the entrenched secularism and massive changes that will characterize the early twenty-first century. The answer for Christian leadership is the church's vision as found in the Scriptures. According to chapter 4, a church's vision is a clear, challenging picture of the future of its ministry as it believes it can and must be. How does it relate to Scripture?

Some suggest that this concept of vision is what the writer is addressing in Proverbs 29:18. I believe that it is and it is not. The Hebrew word translated "vision" in the King James Version of Proverbs 29:18 is better translated "revelation" in the New International Version. It is explained in the second or parallel portion of the text as "the law." Consequently, the vision referred to in this passage is a revelation or word from God. Thus it cannot be limited to an institutional vision as defined in chapter 4. However, it certainly includes the definition, because ultimately an organizational ministry vision must come from God as found in his Word. Haddon Robinson writes, "Since our vision must be God's vision, we must gain it from the Scriptures."[1]

Therefore, God has a predetermined vision for the church that is found in the Scriptures. He did not leave this decision in the hands of each ministry's pastor or its board. According to the Scriptures, the vision is essentially the Great Commission as found in Matthew 28:19–20, Mark 16:15, Luke 24:47–48, and Acts 1:8. This is also the church's mission. The difference is that all churches should have the Great Commission as their mission statement. The vision is also the Great Commission, but it reflects the uniqueness of each church in its particular community across America.

While the church's vision is the Great Commission, this raises a second question, What is the Great Commission? The Great Commission mandate consists of three components that unfold chronologically.

The Pursuit of Lost People

America was largely a churched culture in the 1950s. On Sunday morning, most self-respecting people were in church.[2]

It was the culturally correct thing to do. A church could simply place a "Visitors Welcome" sign out in front of its facility and attract a crowd. The problem is that far too many churches today are still ministering as if they are living in the 1950s. Consequently, they have adopted a passive approach of waiting for people, even lost people, to come to them rather than going after them. As a result, many of these churches are empty and dying in the unchurched culture of the 1990s. The first component of the Great Commission is the intentional pursuit of people, particularly lost people. It is found in the term *go* in Matthew 28:19, "Therefore go and make disciples of all nations, baptizing them in the name of the Father and of the Son and of the Holy Spirit." It is repeated in Mark 16:15, "He said to them, 'Go into all the world and preach the good news to all creation.'" In these two passages, Christ is exhorting his church to pursue or seek lost people.[3] This invasion mentality is both commanded and modeled by the Savior in the first century and is meant to characterize his church in the twenty-first century.

Pursuing Lost People in the First Century

The intentional pursuit of lost people is a common theme in the Gospels. In particular, Luke develops this theme in several places in his Gospel. The first is Luke 5:27–32. In this section, Levi the tax collector has come to faith through the ministry of the Savior. He, in turn, invites his lost friends to a banquet for the purpose of introducing them to the Messiah. The scribes and Pharisees observe this and strongly criticize the Savior for attending and befriending sinners. Regardless, Jesus went to the banquet demonstrating that lost people matter to God. While he did not accept their sin, Jesus did accept them and pursued them, in contrast to the religious crowd who did neither.

A second reference is Luke 15:1–10. In verses 1–2, the Pharisees and teachers of the law are heavily criticizing Christ because he ate with tax collectors and sinners, something no self-respecting religious Jew would ever do. Liefeld writes, "In OT times it was taken for granted that God's people did not consort with sinners . . . , (cf. Ps. 1), but the Pharisees extended this beyond the biblical intent. To go so far as to 'welcome' them especially to 'eat' with them, implying table fellowship, was unthinkable to the Pharisees."[4]

Jesus responds to the accusations with several parables. The first is the parable of the lost sheep found in verses 1–7. It concerns a shepherd who is missing only one of one hundred sheep, but he pursues the animal until he finds it. In the analogy, the shepherd is Jesus and the lost sheep represents tax collectors and sinners. Again, the point is that lost people matter so much to God that the Savior is willing to pursue them until he finds them. The same is true of the parable of the lost coin, where a woman loses only one coin but searches for it until she finds it (vv. 8–10).

A third reference is found in Luke 19:1–10. The Savior summarizes this section in verse 10: "For the Son of Man came to seek and to save what was lost." This verse lays bare the Savior's heart. If he was to appear in bodily form and you took his pulse, you would feel this passage pulsating through his veins and arteries. Liefeld writes that "Verse 10 could well be considered the 'key verse' of Luke. . . . The verse itself expresses the heart of Jesus' ministry as presented by Luke, both his work of salvation and his quest for the lost."[5] To understand verse 10 is to grasp the message of Luke.

Most important in this passage are the two infinitives *to seek* and *to save*. They reveal the structure of the section and divide it into two parts. The first is the seeking section (vv. 1–7) where Zacchaeus is pursuing the Savior (v. 3), but, more important, the Savior is seeking him (v. 5) in line with the theme of the Gospel. The second is the saving section (vv. 8–9).

While all of these passages have several factors in common, one relates to the kind of people who are pursued. In each case, they are not the religious people of the first century but those who for various reasons found themselves outside the religious establishment. They are described by Luke as tax collectors and sinners. These are the nonchurched, or more accurately the nontempled, people of the first century.

Pursuing Lost People in the Twenty-First Century

Not only did the Savior pursue lost, nontempled people in the first century, but his church must seek lost, unchurched people in the twenty-first century. The church must consider several factors in accomplishing this mission.

First, America has become predominantly an unchurched culture. Whereas church attendance and membership were expected in the 1950s whether or not one was a Christian, today all that has changed. As mentioned earlier, George Gallup conducted a survey in 1988 of unchurched people in America and discovered that 44 percent of all American adults (age eighteen or older) were unchurched.[6] Peter Wagner estimates that at the beginning of the 1990s the number of nonchurched people was around 55 percent.[7] Most recently, the figure has climbed to approximately 60 percent according to some sources.[8] A pastor friend in Arlington, Texas, (a bedroom community located between Dallas and Fort Worth) indicates that the figure in his community is closer to 90 percent. Several Southern Baptist church planters in the suburbs of Houston, Texas, confirm this figure for their communities as well.

Commenting on this shift, Kennon Callahan writes, "Statistical research, analysis of this culture, and long-range projections all clearly indicate that ours is no longer a churched culture. Study after study and the steady decline of many mainline denominations confirm this fact. We are clearly and decisively entering the mission field of the 1990s."[9]

Second, the church in America must pursue this lost generation. Prior to the shift in the culture, most evangelism was conducted within the four walls of the church facility. Again,

111

it was easier because the custom was for Christian and non-Christian people to attend church. "Within the broad-based culture after World War II, people held the value that church was important. There was a commonly held belief that participation in church helped one to live a good life. Newcomers, when they moved into a community, were asked, 'What church do you belong to? We want to invite you to visit our church.' People sought the church out and self-initiated their own participation. It was 'the thing to do' to go to church."[10]

Today this is the exception rather than the rule. Thus, the evangelical church must adopt an invasion mentality. It must intentionally and aggressively pursue nonchurched people if it is to accomplish the Great Commission vision in its community in this generation. Much as salt and light in Matthew 5:13–14, the church is to penetrate and illumine the culture. This is not as difficult as some imagine. Lost people are not unchurched because they are angry with the church or have an antichurch mentality. Callahan observes, "In an unchurched culture, people do not necessarily view the church as harmful or hurtful. Rather people simply view the church as not particularly relevant or helpful."[11] They would prefer to be elsewhere on Sunday morning: in bed asleep, at the ball game, at work, with the family, and so on.

In fact, the 1988 Gallup survey as mentioned in chapter 3 revealed that today's younger, unchurched generation is most interested in spiritual matters.

> But while the number of "belongers" has declined over the past decade, the number of "believers" has actually increased. The percentage of adults who believe Jesus Christ is God or the Son of God increased from 78 percent in 1978 to 84 percent in 1988; the percentage of those who say they have made a "commitment" to Christ increased from 60 to 66 percent. While these changes are modest, they are significant because Gallup trend surveys have shown that levels of belief and commitment tend to change at a very slow rate.[12]

Gallup is citing the responses of people who are involved in a telephone survey. When an unknown person states over the phone that they believe that Jesus Christ is God or the Son of God, this could mean anything. It does not mean that 84 percent of the population is evangelical or even Christian. However, it does mean that a considerable number of people are interested in spiritual things; therefore, the decade of the 1990s and the early twenty-first century must be viewed as a time of unprecedented opportunity for evangelism in America.

Some of these unchurched Boomers will come back for another look at the church. This often occurs after a marriage and especially when the couple starts a family. Gallup refers to this as the "life cycle effect" and explains that young people often leave the church in their late teens or early twenties but may return in their late twenties.[13] Regarding this effect, George Barna writes that "millions of Boomers were driven by a desire to raise their youngsters with some formal religious education. Toward that end, they temporarily suspended their own concerns about churches and came back to the fold, primarily for the sake of their offspring."[14]

Some believe that Baby Boomers are now returning to the church in large numbers.[15] George Gallup does not see a return in record numbers but predicts a slow return and that within the next five years more than a third will increase their attendance in church.[16] Barna both agrees and disagrees. He acknowledges that Baby Boomers have been returning to the church in record numbers until the last few years. Now he feels the pendulum has swung again in the opposite direction.

Being rational people, though, Boomers also constantly analyze their environment and compare the benefits received against the costs incurred. After a few years of gathering the information necessary to draw a conclusion, the verdict is now in. The Church is guilty of irrelevance. Kids or no kids, literally hundreds of thousands of Boomers are exiting.

The aberrant child-bearing patterns of the generation—and a steady stream of Boomers who dropped out of the Church from 1965–1980, and are now flowing back to religious institutions—have protected some churches from this effect. The reason why things are at a crisis point now is that the balance has shifted: there are now more leaving than there are newly returning.[17]

Regardless of whether they come back or not, the church's mission is now and always has been to pursue people whoever and wherever they are. Just as the Savior spent much time with Levi, Zacchaeus, and the lost, untempled generation of the first century, so churches that significantly impact the twenty-first century will spend time with the lost, unchurched Boomers and Busters of this and future generations.

However, for revival to take place, established churches will need not only to plant churches but to make some significant changes. This does not mean that they must change *what* they believe (biblical principles) but *how* they practice what they believe (cultural practices and programs).[18] As the church approaches the third millennium, it must be willing to flex in its cultural customs and practices to become more relevant and pursue a lost, dying generation of Baby Boomers and Busters for Christ.

The Evangelism of Lost People

The second component of the Great Commission is evangelism. Christ says, "Go into all the world and preach the good news to all creation" (Mark 16:15). The 1980s and the early 1990s have not been the best of times for evangelism in America. Floyd Bartel writes that "95% of all Christians in North America will not win one person to Christ in their entire lifetime."[19] Barna warns, "In the past seven years, the proportion of adults who have accepted Christ as their personal Savior (34%) has not increased."[20] Projections for the future are not encouraging either. In 1990, the leaders of thirty-three American denominations met in Chicago to publicize their plan to start 36,000 churches in the decade of the 1990s. If this goal is fully realized, it will net an average annual growth rate of only 2 percent. Dan Griffiths states that this figure represents "one of the slowest rates of growth for evangelical churches anywhere in the world."[21] Apparently, the typical evangelical churches across this nation have lost a passion for winning lost people to Christ.

By way of contrast, a church with a Great Commission vision makes evangelism a high priority. Its people are not only seeking and relating to lost people, they are reaching lost people. These churches are growing not because Christians are transferring from other churches (transfer growth) but because they are reaching out to lost, unchurched people (conversion growth). Several characteristics distinguish Great Commission churches from most typical churches in the area of evangelism.

The Style of Evangelism

People in typical evangelical churches wrongly view evangelism as exclusively and stereotypically confrontational and often adversarial. This may not be a problem for those who are gifted in this style of evangelism, but they often make up only about 5 to 10 percent of the people in a church. Those who fear confrontation dislike this style and often do not share their faith with lost people. In fact, Donald Posterski warns: "The emergence of a pluralistic culture has serious consequences for determining what are acceptable methods of evangelism. Confrontational styles of witnessing were never popular, but today they are considered offensive. The claim that there was only one way to God was at least marketable in the past, but in today's milieu it is repulsive."[22] This is not entirely true. There is a socioeconomic factor—

115

confrontational evangelism is still effective with some people. Regardless, there is validity in other styles of evangelism. The evangelistic style of Great Commission churches is diverse. First, their people are quick to make friends with lost people. They value unbelievers. They sincerely believe that unsaved people matter to God and are willing to relate to them in their natural networks. When someone takes a snapshot of them and their friends, several lost people appear in the photo.

Next, these churches realize that their people have various styles of evangelism according to each member's unique divine design. Bill Hybels illustrates well this concept. In response to a single, stereotypical style of evangelism, he writes,

> How can we counter it? By understanding that there are many styles of effective evangelism. In fact, there are probably as many effective styles as there are evangelists.
>
> Only a tiny fraction of the unbelievers in this world will be reached by the stereotypical evangelist. The unbelieving world is made up of a variety of people: young and old, rich and poor, educated and uneducated, urban and rural, with different races, personalities, values, political systems, and religious backgrounds. Isn't it obvious it would take more than one style of evangelist to reach such a diverse population?[23]

Hybels identifies six different evangelistic styles in the Scriptures.[24] The first is a *confrontational style* as used by Peter in Acts 2. Hybels writes, "Some people will only come to Christ if they are 'knocked over the head with truth' and confronted by someone like Peter."[25] The second is an *intellectual style* used by Paul in Acts 17, which involved reasoning with Jews and God-fearing Greeks from the Scriptures, "explaining and proving that Christ had to suffer and rise from the dead." The third is a *testimonial*, which was demonstrated in John 9 where Jesus healed the man blind from birth. When questioned by others, the man testified, "One thing I do know. I was blind but now I see!" (John 9:25). A fourth is a *relational style* found in Mark 5. Here Jesus casts a demon out of a man who then desires to live with the Savior. Instead, Jesus tells him, "Go home to your family and tell them how much the Lord has done for you, and how he has had mercy on you" (Mark 5:19). The point is that he is to go and share with his family and friends. The fifth is an *invitational style* illustrated in John 4 by the conversion of the Samaritan woman. After trusting in the Savior, she went back to her people and invited them to come hear Jesus (vv. 28–29). The sixth style is *service*. Dorcas models this style of evangelism in Acts 9 through her acts of kindness.

The importance of this multistyle approach to evangelism is twofold. First, the focus is on people, not programs. Too many churches that desire to become involved in evangelism first adopt a specific program and then attempt to fit their people into that program. The best approach is to start with people and adopt the program or programs that best serve them. Therefore, people take priority over programs. Second, people who witness on the basis of their natural style do so with authenticity. To attempt evangelism by adopting a style foreign to one's design violates that authenticity and sets that person up for failure, and their rejection ratio is high.

The Motive

A second characteristic of Great Commission churches is motive. The motive for evangelism in many typical churches is guilt. If people share the gospel, it is not because they want to but because they feel they have to out of guilt. This is due most often to the efforts of a well-meaning pastor who wants his people to share their faith but does not understand the implications of motivation by guilt. The result of this approach is that people not only fail to share their faith, but they suffer emotionally. Eventually, they reach a point where they walk away from church and join the ranks of the unchurched.

The motives in Great Commission churches are those championed by John Stott in *Our Guilty Silence*. He presents three from the greater to the lesser. The first is gratitude that flows from our love for Christ. The second is loving concern for men, and the third is loving obedience to God and Christ.[26] These mature people are excited about what Christ has done, and they want to see others come to know him and experience that same joy. They believe that Christianity is not simply a better way to live but that it is the only way to live.

The Method

A third characteristic is method. Most typical churches that even attempt evangelism employ one or possibly two methods. It is most common to hear an evangelistic sermon followed by an altar call. Others rely on Good News Clubs or Awana programs. Great Commission churches involve numerous methods in their attempts at reaching the lost. They may use an evangelistic sermon—some even utilize the altar call. But most employ a variety of methods including various evangelistic children's programs, evangelistic home Bible studies, seeker services, small-group recovery programs, and so on.

The Messenger

A fourth characteristic is the messenger. Our society is in desperate need of authentic disciples who display a passion for the Savior. They are by no means perfect people, but people of integrity who are in process. In *Reinventing Evangelism*, Donald Posterski writes, "We need to become Christian meaning-makers. Meaning-makers are people who make sense of life, people who make sense of God, people whose lives ring with clarity in the midst of contemporary ambiguity, people who have integrity, people who reside in today's world revealing with their living and their lips that Jesus' death is the source of vital life."[27]

The Edification of Saved People

The final component of the Great Commission is edification. Great Commission churches are not evangelistic headhunters. Their goal is to make disciples—to see ungodly pagans become completely committed Christians with a passion for Christ. They do not reach lost people only to later drop them, but they work hard at enfolding and discipling them with the goal of Christlikeness, (see Eph. 4:11–16). They are determined to see deciders become disciples. In short, they take responsibility for their fruit. This edification or sanctification process involves various elements that are realized within a structure.

The Elements

Many of the elements that make up the edification process are found in the life of the early church as pictured in Acts 2:42–47. These same elements are found in today's Great Commission churches. First, they teach new believers the Scriptures (see v. 42). Peter writes that Christians are to crave pure spiritual milk, so that by it they may grow up in their salvation (see 1 Pet. 2:2). According to 1 Peter 1:24–25, this spiritual milk consists at least in part of good Bible teaching. But teaching involves much more than the communication of biblical content, it includes living it as well. The road to spiritual maturity is not Bible knowledge but *applied* Bible knowledge. Therefore, James admonishes Christians to be doers of the word as well as hearers (see James 1:22). In Matthew 7:24–28, the Savior concludes the Sermon on the Mount with the story of the wise and foolish builders. The wise builders are those who having heard Christ's word have chosen to practice it in their lives.

Second, they encourage new Christians to fellowship with other more seasoned Christians who are following Christ (see Acts 2:42). It is critical that new believers see what it is they are to become. Therefore, they need Christlike models (see 1 Cor. 11:1). However, this does not argue that they cut themselves off from any contact with non-Christians. That is a false view of separation. How will they reach lost people if they do not know any? Christ's high-priestly prayer in John 17 was not for his people to stay out of the world. It concerned their being *in* the world but not *of* the world. According to many pastors, the problem for Christianity in the 1990s is that too many professing Christians are *of* the world and not *in* the world. The result is that Christianity loses on both counts.

Third, they lead new converts to worship God (see Acts 2:47). According to Romans 12:1–2, an important aspect of commiting one's self to the service of Christ is worship. Christ's church makes a big mistake if it ignores the emotional aspect of its people. Worship, and particularly the music in worship, involves people in knowing God not only with their minds but with their hearts. Good worship accomplishes both. It starts with the mind in terms of its content but does not stop there. It proceeds to touch the emotions and move one's total being toward adoration and commitment to Christ.

This can take place with either a contemporary or a traditional worship format. Christ's churches must be sensitive to the people who prefer traditional worship while remaining open to those who prefer contemporary worship. Often new converts prefer the latter. In some contexts, both styles can be blended in the same service. In others, it is preferable to have two separate services. If this is not possible, then established, traditional churches must become involved in planting churches that provide more contemporary worship alternatives. In addition, other elements are part of the edification process. Acts 2:42 mentions the breaking of bread (probably the Lord's Supper) and prayer.

The Structure

Great Commission churches also provide opportunities for new converts to meet in both large- and small-group contexts much as the early church in Acts 2:46, 5:42, and probably 20:20. The large-group meetings provide a good context for the body to come together for corporate evangelism, preaching, teaching, and worship. Something special, almost indescribable, takes place when believers gather together in significant numbers to honor God. It takes place when seminary and college students meet in a chapel service; it takes place at a Billy Graham rally in a packed stadium. In commenting on worship in a large group, Peter Wagner writes, "When a lot of people come together, hungry to meet God, a special kind of worship experience can occur. That experience is what I want to call 'celebration.'" In trying to capture this experience, he compares it to that of a sporting event, "As every sports fan knows there is something about a game played before seventy-five thousand spectators that makes it superior to the same game played before fifteen hundred."[28]

The small-group meetings provide the best context for life change. Far too many churches at the end of the twentieth century depend entirely upon the Sunday sermon to catalyze transformation in people's lives. This places too great a burden on the ministry of the pulpit. Most people come to faith in Christ or a commitment to a lifetime of service not as the result of an event such as preaching, but as the result of a relationship that is cultivated in a mentoring or small-group context. Consequently, as many Great Commission churches prepare for ministry in the twenty-first century, they are asking the question, Should small-group ministry be simply another program of the church, or the way the church does its ministry? Though far too many churches hire their pastors to do the work of the ministry, the Bible teaches that certain gifted people are to train the church to do the work of the ministry (Eph. 4:11–12).

121

In essence, the pastor passes the ministry baton to his people, and the structure that best facilitates lay ministry that brings life change is the small group.

Food for Thought

1. In what sense are the mission and vision statements of the church the same? In what ways are they different?
2. In what sense is the concept of vision found in Proverbs 29:18 different from the organizational vision defined in chapter 4? How are they alike?
3. The church's vision is the Great Commission. What is the Great Commission? Is the heart of your church's vision the Great Commission? If not, why?
4. What do lost people at the end of the twentieth century have in common with lost people of the first century?
5. How would you answer the question, Are the Baby Boomers returning to church?
6. What is the difference between a church's forms and its functions? Give some examples of each.
7. What is your style of evangelism? Is your style one of the six listed in this chapter? Is confrontation evangelism easy for you? Why or why not?
8. Review the circumstances surrounding your conversion and your commitment to follow Christ. Were they the result of an event (preaching) or a relationship (a mentor or small group)?

6

Planting Churches
Birthing Robust Babies

* Where does the Bible refer to church planting? Does Scripture display any examples of planted churches?
* At what time in the nation's history did most church planting take place—at the nation's birth, between the Civil War and World War II, or at the end of the twentieth century?
* What is the current attitude of the American church toward church planting? Is your church interested in birthing new congregations?
* What might be some objections to parenting churches?

The 1960s proved to be a cultural shock—a period of extreme turbulence that exacted a heavy toll on the very soul of America. The nation convulsed under the assassinations of two Kennedys and Martin Luther King, Jr., the moral revolution involving an increase of sexual promiscuity, the unpopular Vietnam War that resulted in the death of fifty thousand young Americans, the emergence of the civil rights movement, the increase of urban riots, and the rise of the counterculture and strong antiestablishment views on the part of America's youth. At the same time, Jesus

Christ was busy bringing a large number of young people to himself through a revival popularly labeled the Jesus Movement.

In particular, the Savior used the leadership of Chuck Smith and the ministry of Calvary Chapel to win large numbers of young people, including society's dropouts, to the gospel. God moved in his heart and that of his wife, Kay, to love and reach out to those who were either not interested in or had largely been rejected by the traditional churches of that era. Preaching often in tents and along the California coast to young people and beaded, bearded hippies, Smith baptized multitudes in the Pacific Ocean. The spiritual impact on those lives has been phenomenal. Today Calvary Chapel of Costa Mesa, California, continues to have a vibrant ministry that has in excess of three hundred affiliate congregations across America, many of which are pastored by those former societal dropouts.

America in the 1990s and the early third millennium faces many problems that are holdovers from the 1960s as well as other perplexing problems that have accumulated over the last few decades of emerging secularism. Entrenched secularism represents a major challenge to the American church as it rapidly approaches the twenty-first century. Clearly, reaching out to this secular nation in an intentional way with a powerful Great Commission vision will prove most difficult. The development of a profound vision is not enough, however. The church must begin to think and move toward new paradigms for ministry.

God continues to work quietly behind the scenes raising up exciting Great Commission churches to reach out to a secular, troubled nation. What many fail to realize is that for the most part these high-impact ministries have been planted churches. After experiencing so much decline and death, the future of the American church is church planting.[1]

The Importance of Church Planting

The critical importance of church planting to the future of the church in America is easily demonstrated from the Scriptures and the nation's history.

The Biblical Importance

Birthing new churches is biblical. For an evangelical who holds to biblical authority, the temptation is to stop here and say, "Enough said—end of discussion." The fact that starting churches is solidly based on Scripture is more than sufficient reason for the multiplication of new works to those who believe in the inerrancy of the Bible. However, it must be demonstrated that this premise is true. The biblical evidence is twofold.

The Book of Acts. The first piece of evidence is found in the Book of Acts. As stated earlier, according to Matthew 28:19–20 and Mark 16:15, the church's mission and vision from the Savior is the Great Commission. It consists of three elements: the pursuit, the evangelization, and the discipling of lost people. The Great Commission mission encompasses what the church is all about—it is Christ's marching orders for the church. But it is important to ask, How did the early church understand and implement Christ's vision? The answer is well documented in the Book of Acts, the church history book of the New Testament.

Most often the Book of Acts is viewed from a missions perspective. In fact, a missions curriculum at any Christian school or church that does not include a study of the emerging church in Acts is decidedly deficient. Various texts and commentaries on Acts usually emphasize the missions component. However, the fact that Acts is all about church planting must not be lost or unintentionally ignored in the process. A careful study of the book indicates that the early church implemented the Great Commission mandate through planting churches.

In Acts 2, God reveals the church, a new people of God, which is the body of Christ (see Col. 1:18) that includes both Jews and Gentiles (see Eph. 2:11–22). After the planting of the church in Jerusalem, Phoenicia, Cyprus, and Antioch (see Acts 2–12) the rest of the book records the spread of Christianity to various parts of the world through planting new bodies of believers on three separate missionary journeys (see Acts 13–28).

The first missionary or church planting trip is found in Acts 13:1–14:28. It records the birthing of local churches in such key cities as Antioch, Iconium, Lystra, and Derbe located primarily in Asia Minor (modern-day Turkey). The second journey is in Acts 15:36–18:22. It records church plants in the strategic cities of Phillipi, Thessalonica, Berea, Athens, and Corinth, which show the extension of the church beyond Asia Minor into what is now Greece. The final excursion is in Acts 18:23–21:26. Luke describes what may have included the planting of some churches in Asia Minor and Greece but was primarily a journey to strengthen the churches planted on the second trip. And Acts 19:21–28:31 records the events that lead eventually to the planting of the church in Rome and beyond.

Romans 15:20. In the midst of his concluding remarks to the Christian community in Rome that stretches from Romans 15:14 to the end of the book, Paul makes reference to the geographical coverage of his life's ministry, which extended "from Jerusalem all the way around to Illyricum" (Rom. 15:19). Next, he pauses to share with them his passion. "It has always been my ambition to preach the gospel where Christ was not known . . ." (v. 20).

The idea is that Paul was a pioneer church planter in the truest sense. He pushed through what was virgin territory in terms of the gospel to plant churches to reach new people for Christ "so that I might not be building on someone else's foundation" (Rom. 15:20). His point is that his passion is for starting churches rather than building up that which another has started.

1 Corinthians 3:5–10. Here Paul alludes to his passion for initiating churches. In verse 10 he describes himself as an expert builder who begins a work by laying the foundation. His ministry goal was entrepreneurial—to plant new churches and then turn them over to another who would build them up.

The Historical Importance

Birthing new churches is not only biblical, it is historical. It has proved vital to the spread of Christianity across America in its past history and is critical to its future.

Church planting in the past.[2] Contrary to the opinion of some, America did not begin as a strong Christian nation. Paulus Scharpff writes, "In 1790, when the population of the United States was approximately four million, only five percent of the population belonged to any church."[3] It was during the half century from the Civil War to the beginning of World War I that America's mainline denominations recorded strong growth due to the planting of a significant number of churches (see table 5). In 1820, eleven thousand Protestant congregations existed with an American population of 9.6 million people. That is a ratio of one church for every 875 people. In 1860, the number of congregations grew to fifty-four thousand, while the population increased to 31.5 million—a ratio of one church for every 610 people. Finally, in 1906, the number of churches climbed to 212,000, and the population grew to 85.4 million—a ratio of one church for every 430 people.[4] Consequently, the key to evangelism during this period proved to be the planting of hundreds of thousands of new churches. In reviewing these statistics, Schaller concludes, "It continues to be the most useful and productive component of any denominational church growth strategy."[5]

However, Schaller notes a statistical change from the turn of the century to the 1980s (see table 6). Between 1899 and 1906, the population increased by 9 million people and the number of new churches increased by thirty-two thousand, for a ratio of one church for every 280 additional people. But from 1980 to 1989, while the population increased twenty-four million people, the number of new churches was only thirty-five thousand, which is a ratio of one church for every 685 additional people in the population.[6]

Table 5

Year	Number of Churches	U.S. Population	Ratio
1820	11,000	9.6 million	1/875
1860	54,000	31.5 million	1/610
1906	212,000	85.4 million	1/430

Table 6

Years	Number of New Churches	Population Increase	Ratio
1899–1906	32,000	9 million	1/280
1980–1989	35,000	24 million	1/685

At the same time, the denominational churches continued to increase in size. Schaller writes, "Between 1906 and 1970 the average (mean) size of the congregations in several denominations doubled or tripled."[7] As demonstrated in chapter 2, much of this growth took place in the 1950s. However, in the 1960s denominational leaders shifted their priorities away from planting churches to programs for social and economic justice.[8] Since that time and even before, the old-line Protestant churches have experienced an unprecedented membership decline that is documented and developed in chapter 2.

While it might prove difficult to demonstrate a direct cause-and-effect relationship, it does appear that the growth of the churches between 1906 and 1970 only temporarily offset the lack of church planting that was evident beginning in the 1960s. The full brunt of this has been experienced in the major decline of the mainline denominations since the 1960s to the present. A reasonable conclusion, therefore, is that the birthing of new churches is the key to the growth and spread of Christianity in America.

Church planting in the future. The historical evidence indicates that while America did not begin as a strong Christian nation, the church and its Christian influence did grow until it peaked in the 1950s and since then has declined. Win Arn writes, "In the years following World War II thousands of new churches were established. Today, of the approximately 350,000 churches in America, four out of the five are either plateaued or declining. . . . In the normal life cycle of churches, there is birth, and in time, death. Many churches begin a plateau and/or slow decline around their 15th–18th year." Then he offers a staggering statistic for the current state of the church: "80–85 % of the churches in America are on the down-side of this growth cycle."[9] His point is that the American church is in the midst of a serious decline. I have argued in chapter 2 that this decline has affected today's evangelical churches as well as the mainline denominations.

This raises again the question, What is the future of the church in America? Is it rapidly becoming a thing of the past? Except for a few scattered congregations, will it disappear? I have answered this question in chapter 3, where I argue that the future could see a major revival. This is due primarily to Matthew 16:18 where the Savior, forseeing times such as these, promises that the church will survive any and all satanic assaults against it.

However, based on the historical evidence from the past, birthing new congregations will be the key to authentic evangelism and spiritual revival. Peter Wagner concurs, "The single most effective evangelistic methodology under heaven is planting new churches."[10] It is unrealistic to believe that today's struggling established churches can accomplish evangelism and revival without planting churches. Schaller calls attention to the fact that most churches in the United States reach a peak in size during their first twenty or thirty years and then either plateau or shrink in size. The reasoning is that while most begin with an outward focus, in time, they turn inward, allocating their resources and their attention on the maintenance of the organization and the care of the membership.[11]

A Strategy for Church Planting

The Problem

It is evident that church planting is the critical element in a national strategy for reaching out to and influencing America in the 1990s and the third millennium. There is a critical need to plant different kinds of churches to reach different kinds of people. Otherwise, we will not reach Bobby, LaTonya, or Brian. The problem is that too few churches in America are even thinking about birthing new churches much less doing it. While numerous reasons exist for their lack of interest, I have included five.

1. *Ignorance.* Some congregations remain unaware of the current state of church decline. Many of these are plateaued churches that still have enough people entering the front door of the church to offset the number exiting the back door. They can pay the bills, which has become a high priority in difficult economic times. Many of them are located in the South and the Bible Belt where numerous church buildings still decorate the major streets and downtown areas of the city. People who drive by these impressive structures feel a certain confidence in the future of the American church that

would quickly evaporate should they ever stop on a Sunday and visit the aging and dwindling congregations that are housed within.

2. *Revitalization.* Some churches are aware of the problems facing the church in the 1990s and beyond. However, they believe the best strategy is to revitalize the established churches first. Once this is accomplished, then it will be time to plant new congregations. The slogan is: "Let's put first things first." While church revitalization is a viable strategy (and the topic of the next chapter), it must take place at the same time as church planting. The hard truth is that revitalizing new churches involves much energy and large infusions of change, and many established churches will find that they are tired and that it is too painful to make the kinds of changes necessary for revival. Those that are willing to make the changes, especially those that are on a plateau, will discover that revitalization does not happen overnight. It can be a long, time-consuming process. Consequently, revitalization of churches is important, but it must take place in conjunction with church planting.

3. *Survival.* Some churches will not consider starting new congregations because they have a survival mentality. In these days of decline they find themselves too busy trying to maintain the current programs. It is all they can do to keep their doors open from Sunday to Sunday. The very thought of birthing a church strikes them with the fear of losing what they have strived for so many years to maintain.

The problem is that many of these survivalist churches are having virtually no impact on the community. A number are located in areas where the community has changed and the current membership consists of those not living in the community but who have moved out to the suburbs and are driving in to attend services each Sunday.

The solution to their problem is twofold and involves church planting. First, the church could sell or give their facility to a core group (preferably one that is homogeneous with the people in that area) for the purpose of starting a church at the present site and use any proceeds to start a new church in another area. Second, they could sell their facility to the highest bidder and then use the funds to plant a church in another part of the city. The difficulty with this approach is that the old church with all its wonderful memories dies, and few want to take part in pronouncing the last rites. Therefore, it is important that the old congregation view the death of the church as necessary to give birth to new life.

4. *Finances.* Some will not consider church planting because they believe that the start-up costs are too high. They are convinced that it takes a lot of money to plant churches well. Conventional wisdom teaches that it is better not to attempt it without sufficient funding.

This objection may or may not be true depending on the kind of church one is planting and where that church is to be located. Those who desire to plant a seeker-driven type of church like Willow Creek Community Church near Chicago, Illinois, will need significant funding up-front, especially those that employ high-quality musicians, a well-designed, high-impact mail campaign, or a telephone program such as "The Phones for You."[12] These churches believe in high quality—if it is worth doing, then it is worth doing well. Others, however, may not need large infusions of capital, especially those that start with a small-group or cell approach to church planting. Regardless, Peter Wagner writes, "The truth of the matter is that in terms of dollars spent by the sponsoring church or agency, new church planting can be the most cost effective method of evangelization."[13]

One of the difficulties for churches in funding multiple congregations is that the results are not always apparent. When a church spends money on itself such as a new addition, a brand new building, a new vehicle, or another staff person, people see and appreciate more what their money has accomplished. Investing in a daughter church is less obvious. If the church plant shares the same facility (as is the case with many ethnic churches), people are more aware of their investment but may sometimes respond negatively due to ethnocentrism. If the church meets elsewhere in the community, out of sight becomes out of mind, and less value is placed on the new ministry. The solution to this problem is vision casting. The congregation must see in their heads what they cannot see with their eyes.

5. *Vision.* Some churches have not considered starting new congregations because they lack vision for outreach. Their vision only goes as far as their own church—they cannot see past it to their secularized community nor to a world in desperate need. Many of these are maintenance ministries that are growing or have recently plateaued. Some are in the midst of building programs or are trying to overcome the debt incurred as the result of having recently completed a new facility or addition.

On occasion, individuals within the church will approach the leadership about birthing a daughter in the community using some of the members as a core group. This happened in Dallas, Texas, when a recent seminary graduate approached a Bible church about starting a new work in the area. The senior pastor and his board were quick to let him know that they were adamant against losing any sources of income or workers either now or in the future. In essence, they were committed to building their own little kingdom and would emotionally beat up anyone who threatened it. In spite of their opposition, the young entrepreneur planted a church that is reaching out to a different group of younger people with a different ministry menu.

The result of the lack of interest in multiplying congregations on the part of so many churches has several dire consequences. One is the lack of evangelistic outreach to the community. Again, the best strategy to saturate a community with the gospel is to salt it with new churches. Another is that the church fails to reap the benefits that accrue, such as a sense that something exciting is happening—God is doing something special through this body. Perhaps the greatest consequence is that many church planters will attempt to start new works by themselves, which, in turn, dramatically increases their chances of failure.

The Solution

The solution to the problem is more churches with a passion to plant daughter churches—America needs more parent churches! Rather than sit back and bemoan the fact that America is a post-Christian nation, Christ's churches across the land need to view the situation more positively and see the country as pre-Christian, much like the early church in the first century, and in need of numerous new churches.

In the late 1980s and early 1990s a number of denominations and organizations have awakened to the stranglehold of secularism on American culture and the church. They have also realized the need to parent new churches if they are to exert any spiritual influence on the culture. In fact, there is a growing number of these denominations and organizations who are pushing from the top down to multiply high-impact congregations. While some organizations exist that have not realized the need for planting churches, the problem exists more on the local level. Only so much pressure can be applied from the top; the churches on the grassroots level must catch the vision. They are the critical element to any strategy to reach out to the nation as a whole. Without them, the outreach will be extremely difficult if not impossible.

Some potential mother churches, especially those in the South and the Bible Belt areas of the country, might object. They could argue that America does not need more churches, for a church is present on every corner in their communities. However, as stated earlier in this chapter, 80 to 85 percent of these churches are on a plateau or in decline with little if any outreach. Also, many are still ministering as if they were living in the 1940s or 1950s—they are old paradigm churches. Even those areas of the nation with lots of churches need new paradigm churches (most often newly planted churches) to reach those of a younger generation who have turned a deaf ear to the established church. It will take a new generation of churches to reach a new generation of people.

One disadvantage to the mother church concept needs some discussion. Often new churches tend to model themselves after the parent. A general truth is that it takes different kinds of churches to reach different kinds of people. To copy the parent church may result in a new ministry that is not authentic to the people it is most likely to reach in its target community. Another disadvantage could be a dysfunctional parent church. In *Effective Church Leadership*, Kennon Callahan writes,

> The mother-daughter church modality of starting new congregations has precisely that flaw in it. The mother churches are typically stable and declining churches. The members who leave that mother church to become the founding core of the new daughter church have generally learned how to build a stable and declining church. . . . The new daughter church will experience a blush of growth during the first three to four years because of the newness, the enthusiasm, and the pioneering spirit that attracts persons to a new church. But usually about the fourth or fifth year, the church will bump up against some tough, hard decisions. And in its decision making, it will fall back on the conserving, holding, protecting, preserving behavior patterns of stable and declining churches. It will become preoccupied with the functional characteristics. Like mother, like daughter.[14]

However, the advantages far outweigh the disadvantages, and a number of ways exist in which a mother church can help in the incubation of daughter churches.

Finances. A major problem facing new church starts is funding. It takes finances to survive in this world. Older, established churches must realize that just as it takes significant funding to keep their doors open, so new churches will need some help in this area. The new work faces such funding needs as the support of its full-time ministry personnel, the rental of a facility in which to meet, utilities, costs for advertising, quality sound equipment, and so on. Some planted churches have the vision and momentum to reach an entire community but are slowed in the process because of a lack of funding. While it is generally true that the kind of leaders who make good church planters can often raise much of the necessary support, this takes valuable time away from the church planting project and can prove emotionally draining. Other ways are available to assess a person's ability to lead a church planting team.[15]

This is where understanding mother churches can prove extremely beneficial. They can provide strong financial backing at the start and then scale down their support as the church gradually becomes self-supporting. These funds might come from affluent individuals in the congregation who have caught a vision for church planting, or they could be a permanent part of the church's budget. Another option is to provide a one-time gift up-front to get the new church started. A third option is to present the new work during a service or at a congregational meeting and challenge the people to support it on an individual basis. In a culture characterized by financial mismanagement and the gross misappropriation of funds, the advantage with all these options is that the sponsoring church can hold the new church accountable for its use of the finances.

Core group. Most churches begin as either a "cold start" or a "hot start." A "cold start" involves gathering a nonexistent group of believers into the initial core group. A "hot start" catalyzes and galvanizes a group of Christians who have already come together in some locale for the purpose of planting a church. The advantages of the latter usually outweigh those of the former. Another advantage of a mother church is that it can provide some or all of the people who make up the initial core group in a "hot start."

This could occur in several different scenarios. First, the daughter church may locate in a neighboring community where a pocket of members live who are driving a long distance to attend the mother church. Another scenario is for the home church to loan a core group of members to the new work for as long as it takes to provide the critical mass necessary to attract new people. A third scenario involves recruiting a team of people who are willing to leave home and move to another area to plant a church there.

In any of the above scenarios, the home church provides magnet or attractor people. Jesus calls them "salt and light" people (see Matt. 5:13–14). These are individuals or couples with spiritual, personal, and character qualities that naturally draw people to them. Wherever they live and wherever they go, people are uniquely attracted to them because of their strong people skills that are a part of their natural design from God. Everyone in their neighborhoods regardless of their spiritual condition know them, and the majority speak and think highly of them. When they are strategically placed in new core groups, they experience quick, early growth attracting both Christians and non-Christians.

Accountability. A third advantage is that a sponsoring church can provide necessary accountability for the new work. This affects several areas. The importance of financial accountability was mentioned above. It is important to contributors that they have assurance that their gifts are being used appropriately. People are willing to give sacrificially to support new works but are cautious due to the heavily publicized financial scandals of the televangelists. Another area is moral integrity. The church planting pastor could be viewed as a part of the staff of the home church and held morally accountable to them as they should be to one another. A flaw in moral character would prove fatal to the new work. A third area is the family. Church planters seldom put in less than a forty-hour week. Certainly, birthing new churches is not for the lazy, and it often attracts people who are driven. They must not allow the church family to replace their own families. The staff of the mother church could hold the planter accountable as well as model good family life.

Encouragement. A problem that every leader faces in ministry is discouragement. No one is exempt, particularly church planters—it comes with the territory. Ministry, like the weather, has its rainy days as well as its sunny days. Even Paul, who was a church planter par excellence, faced times of extreme discouragement (see 2 Tim. 4:9–16).

The difficulty is facing discouragement alone. Except for his jailers and Luke, Paul was alone (see vv. 9–11). Here is where the host church can be extremely helpful. The senior pastor and others in the host church can serve as listening ears and through their presence or availability provide comfort and encouragement to see the planter through these difficult periods. In fact, a wise host church might assign a group in the congregation to keep their finger on the pulse of the new church and be ready to assist when they feel any disillusionment pulsating in its veins.

Prayer. Those who plant churches must recruit an intercessory prayer team. Like lungs to the human body, so prayer is the spiritual lungs for the new church body. The real battle in church planting is not the visible warfare that takes place in the physical realm of limited finances, difficult relationships, and so forth, but the invisible warfare that takes place in the spiritual realm (see Eph. 6:10–19). The real reason why many new works abort or die in early childhood is not because of any human factors but rather satanic or demonic opposition. Satan does not want established churches to catch a vision for planting Great Commission churches. According to Ephesians 6:18–19, prayer is one of the primary and most powerful weapons in the Christian's arsenal against Satan and his spiritual forces.

The alert sponsoring church assists the new church by providing intercessory prayer teams that have been recruited, are in place, and are functioning. The church starter may want to recruit a prayer team within the planted church as well, but there will never be a case of *too much* prayer. It is amazing how many obstacles are overcome and what God will accomplish when a faithful body of prayer warriors gets behind the efforts of a new work.

Credibility. In the 1980s and the early 1990s a number of events took place that damaged the credibility of Christianity in a secular culture. Most of us are familiar with the sexual and financial scandals that rocked the popular ministries of certain world-famous televangelists in the 1980s. Then in the early 1990s an extremist, fundamentalist Muslim sect bombed the World Trade Center in New York City. This was followed by the government's siege of the fundamentalist Branch Davidian sect in Waco, Texas, which ended in disaster. These two high media events have focused much negative publicity on anything that hints of religious fundamentalism, even among fundamental and evangelical Christians.

These events pose several questions. How do those in the community or potential members know that the work is not some religious extremist group? Or, How might people discern between the new church and some fly-by-night operation? These are important questions that people will be asking in the 1990s.

Church planting teams without established, reasonably well-known mother churches will have difficulty answering these kinds of questions. One solution is to form a board consisting of credible Christians in the community who endorse and support the new ministry. A better approach is to identify with a sponsoring church that is known for its spiritual integrity and authenticity. The association of the two will provide the new church with instant credibility that would otherwise take some time to earn.

Counsel. One of the problems in ministry in general and church planting in particular is the need to have both the knowledge and wisdom to make good, godly decisions in various ministry situations. In light of a changing culture in a changing world, church planters constantly face critical decisions that can move their ministries forward or set them back. Church planting also, by nature, is a risk-taking venture. This places a tremendous amount of pressure on the lone church planter or the point person on the church planting team that eventually exacts a heavy toll emotionally and spiritually, especially when bad decisions are made.

The counsel of a seasoned pastor and church staff can be of great benefit to the daughter church. Every leader makes mistakes, and good leaders learn from their mistakes. Over time, the leader uses all this to build a knowledge base that is marbled with wisdom. When church planters, who often are younger in age and less experienced, face difficult decisions, they can turn to the pastor or staff of the host church and tap into the years of experience. Scripture is clear concerning the importance of making decisions that are based on good, godly counsel (see Prov. 11:14; 12:15; 15:22; 19:20).

Talent. A serious problem that faces all new churches is the talent problem. This is evident at various times during the life of the church such as the inception and birth stages.[16] Scripture encourages the church by example and commands it to pursue and sustain a reasonable excellence in all that it does (see Lev. 22:20–22; Num. 18:29–30; Eph. 6:5–8; Col. 3:23–24).[17]

This is especially true of worship. Christians who sing off-key (due to lack of effort or failure to rehearse) or play untuned instruments (simply because they did not take the time to tune them) detract from rather than aid the cause of Christ. Visitors and unchurched people view this as inauthentic. They can leave such a service wondering why God is not worthy of people's best efforts and feel that perhaps they should turn to others who take their faith more seriously. They do not understand why people who attempt their very best for an employer five or six days a week cannot attempt their best for God on Sunday morning. A reasonable excellence does not mean that participants do not make mistakes. It does mean, however, that when they do it is not because they were lazy or nonchalant but because they are human.

How can a new church avoid this problem? It is not likely that it will attract talented, gifted people at its inception. It takes time for most churches to recruit and put together this kind of talent. Again, the answer lies with the help of the mother church that is willing to make these people available to the new church. The church that is rich in talent is not able to use all of its people all of the time. Therefore, it could serve well the new church by giving or lending to it these gifted individuals.[18]

Personnel. I strongly promote church planting in a team context.[19] New Testament ministry is clearly a team ministry. Also, solo church planting has a high failure rate. As Lyle Schaller once put it, "Starting a new church is one of the loneliest jobs in the world. I wouldn't do it unless I were part of a team."[20] Regardless, at present much of the church planting taking place in America is accomplished by a team of one. Yet even under the best circumstances—a team context—most new churches tend to be understaffed and inexperienced.

To counteract this problem, the sponsoring church can make their experienced staff available to the new work. The worship leader could advise and be on call to help with the design and implementation of the new worship program. Often a sore point for the new work is a quality program that attracts youth of all ages. The seasoned youth pastor could train and advise those involved in the new church's youth ministry so as to make the best of this situation. Some high-impact, aggressive churches might hire trained people in these areas and loan them to the new ministry until it is up and running.

Some Models for Church Parenting

Who has caught the vision for parenting new churches in America? In spite of the fact that the majority of churches across America in the early 1990s are not thinking about birthing new congregations, notable exceptions exist that provide both a challenging example and a dynamic, working model for what could be and must be in the nation's future. They exist on the denominational or organizational level and the local church level.[21]

Organizational Models

A number of America's denominations and organizations have caught the vision to parent Great Commission churches from sea to shining sea. In 1990, George Barna wrote, "Many denominations have targeted this decade as one for aggressive church planting. If existing plans are carried out, we can expect the number of Protestant churches in America to swell by another 75,000 congregations."[22] The importance of this figure is highlighted by the fact that there are around 260,000 churches in the nation. Pete Wagner adds, "Without exception, the growing denominations have been those that stress church planting. The leaders of these denominations know that church planting is key to their growth, so not only do they believe it themselves, but they see to it that their pastors and lay leaders also believe it."[23] We will look at three of these groups.

The Assemblies of God. One of the fastest growing denominations in America has been the Assemblies of God.[24] Between 1965 to 1985, they grew 116 percent.[25] Unlike so many other denominations, they have decided to pursue people into the 1990s and the twenty-first century. According to the *National and International Religion Report*, their vision for America is "to plant 5,000 new churches, recruit 20,000 new ministers, win 5 million people to Christ, and enlist 1 million people to pray regularly for revival—all by the year 2000."[26] How are they doing? In 1990, they planted 340 new churches—20 percent more than in 1989—and recorded just under 320,000 conversions."[27]

Operating from a base of approximately twelve thousand churches, they are projecting growth in the range of 40 percent. Are they out of their minds? Is this grandiosity at its worst? In Ephesians 3:20, Paul delivers a light slap on the wrist to the church at Ephesus—in essence he writes that God is able to do more than they ask and think. His point: They need to ask (pray) big and think big. The Assemblies of God are doing exactly that. They realize that we have a big God who is more than capable of doing big things. The problem today as in Ephesus is small-thinking people. Should all the denominations catch the same vision, the American church would experience a major revival and deliver a staggering blow to the forces of secularism.

The Southern Baptists. The largest Protestant denomination in America is the Southern Baptists. They are a step ahead of almost everyone else. In 1976 they declared church planting a major emphasis in their challenging and ambitious program called Bold Mission Thrust. Its mission is to tell every person in the United States the story of Jesus and to provide fifty thousand New Testament congregations where new Christians can mature in the faith, can worship, witness, and minister by the year 2000. They envision a church for everyone, which involves more than a church in every geographical location in the States. It means a church for every kind of person according to the targeted community whether African-American, Hispanic, or Anglo.

Early in 1990 they discovered that they were six thousand churches short. Consequently, the Home Mission Board has launched the 15,000 Campaign for the 1990s that will attempt to birth fifteen hundred churches each year to achieve a total of fifteen thousand by the year 2000.[28]

The Evangelical Free Church of America. The Evangelical Free Church was formed in 1950 through the merger of the

Swedish Evangelical Free Church and the Norwegian-Danish Evangelical Free Church Association. Both came into existence during the revival movements of the late nineteenth century. With headquarters in Minneapolis, Minnesota, today it is a movement of more than eleven hundred churches that are committed to planting and multiplying effective, disciplemaking churches. As well as starting churches abroad, their vision is to birth fifteen hundred to two thousand churches in North America in the 1990s.

Building on a foundation of prayer, their strategy includes four critical elements. First, they are actively recruiting two thousand church planters who have a call from God and a vision to reach the unchurched. They include bivocational people, specially trained laypeople, graduates of Bible colleges and seminaries, and pastors of established churches. Second, prospective church planters are assessed to determine God's will for their ministry and placement. The assessment involves a combination of psychological inventories, vocational testing, and interviewing. Third, the EFCA provides special training through Disciplemaking Training Networks (T-NETs), New Church Incubators, and church planter conferences in strategic locations around the nation. Finally, those who successfully complete the assessment program are placed by the district in key areas that are in need of new churches.

Other organizations. In addition to the bold, visionary groups above, other organizations have caught a passion for church planting. The Evangelical Covenant Church historically has begun only ten to twelve churches a year. Their new goal, however, is to double that number to twenty to twenty-five churches before the year 2000, with the aim of receiving two hundred new churches by the year 2002. The Christian and Missionary Alliance, the Church of the Nazarene, the Missionary Church, the Baptist General Conference, and the Church of God (Cleveland) are all making bold moves to birth churches across America during the decade of the 1990s.

Bible colleges and seminaries are also joining the movement. Columbia Biblical Seminary and Graduate School located in Columbia, South Carolina, has been training church planters for years due to their emphasis on world missions. Fuller Theological Seminary offers a doctor of ministry degree in church planting, and most seminaries have at least one course on that subject. Now Dallas Theological Seminary has added to the curriculum a church planting track that focuses on planting churches in the United States or abroad.

Individual Churches

The organizations and denominations above are to be commended for their gallant efforts to seed America and the world with Great Commission churches. Some day they will hear the Father's words, "Well done thou good and faithful servants." However, in most cases they represent a top-down effort. The leadership at the top has caught the vision for church planting. The critical question remains, Will the grassroots churches within these organizations catch the vision as well? And what about all the independent churches that are not part of any denomination or organization—will they develop a passion for supporting or parenting churches?

I am an optimist, and based also on the information in chapter 3, I believe they will. A number of significant, high-impact churches have already caught the vision and provide some outstanding examples and models of parenting for other churches in the 1990s and beyond.

Calvary Chapel of Costa Mesa, California. One exceptional example mentioned earlier is Calvary Chapel of Costa Mesa, California. In 1965 Pastor Chuck Smith of the Foursquare Gospel tradition accepted a call to a church in Santa Ana, California, that had dwindled to twenty-five people. In just a few short years, the church experienced phenomenal growth as a part of the Jesus Movement that won so many young people and ex-hippies to Christ. Smith explains, "We accepted them, and they accepted Christ."[29] In 1971, the church relocated to its present site in Costa Mesa, California, and has over ten thousand families in attendance.

Although he is unassuming and prefers a low profile, Pastor Chuck is a strong Bible teacher with a tremendous vision for the church in America and the world. Presently, Calvary Chapel has either planted, developed, or influenced in excess of three hundred churches in America alone.[30] Affiliate churches are found in every state in the U.S. and in other countries such as Australia, Hong Kong, Mexico, Africa, and China.

Vineyard Christian Fellowship of Anaheim, California. In 1973 Kenn Gullikson began a Bible study that became the first Vineyard Christian Fellowship. Over a period of time this led to the planting of five other Vineyard fellowships in Southern California.

At around the same time in Southern California, due to his emphasis on miraculous healings, John Wimber was asked to leave a Friends assembly. In 1977 he and a group of people from the Friends assembly joined the Calvary Chapel fellowship associated with Chuck Smith, and together they formed the Yorba Linda Calvary Chapel, which grew to more than two thousand members. In 1982 Wimber's ministry became more focused on signs and wonders, so he left the Calvary Chapel fellowship to become a part of Gullikson's Vineyard fellowships.

Almost immediately, Gullikson turned the entire movement over to the leadership of Wimber. Then, in 1983, Wimber relocated the church to Anaheim, California, where it ministers to over five thousand members. With Gullikson serving as church planting consultant for Vineyard Ministries International, Wimber's vision is to aggressively plant ten thousand new Vineyards! Will he accomplish this mission? Already five hundred men have been ordained, and more than three hundred churches exist in the U.S. and Canada.[31]

Wooddale Church of Eden Prairie, Minnesota. Leith Anderson is the senior pastor of Wooddale Church, which is located in the Minneapolis suburb of Eden Prairie, Minnesota. He has led Wooddale over the past ten years through a process of change that has placed it on the cutting edge in terms of churches across America. Not your typical pastor, he combines the talents and abilities of an author, educator, and speaker with his love for ministry in the local church.

Recently, Anderson spoke to my Advanced Church Planting class at Dallas Theological Seminary. In sharing the vision for birthing new churches, he presented the church's aggressive, unselfish approach toward helping new congregations. They use what he terms a "hunting license."

> The basic format is to hire a full-time New Church Pastor who joins the staff of Wooddale Church for six to nine months. During that time of preparation for the start of the new church, the pastor selectively seeks persons with the needed gifts for the new church. This includes teachers, musicians, leaders, contributors, helpers, etc. In many ways, the right gift mix is more important than a large number. Our experience is that it takes about 125 people from Wooddale Church to get the gift mix necessary for a church to be strong from the beginning. These people are recruited by the new pastor. Like a "hunting license" it is for specific people for a specific period of time and with limited numbers.[32]

Anderson's "hunting license" communicates a gracious passion for and strongest of commitments to church planting. How many large, established churches in America would allow a church planter to pursue and take away their gifted teachers, musicians, leaders, and especially financial contributors for another congregation? This approach to new churches articulates a fresh, new spirit toward the birthing ministry. What a decided contrast to those churches that are so worried about losing anyone that they pour lots of cold water all over the slightest spark of entrepreneurial vision.

Saddleback Valley Community Church of Mission Viejo, California. Rick Warren is the founding pastor of Saddleback Church, which is a Southern Baptist ministry located in Mission Viejo just south of Los Angeles. The church began in 1980 with two families and has since grown to over four thousand people in attendance. Rick's passion is to reach non-Christians with the gospel of Christ. Consequently, approximately 70 percent of the Saddleback membership has accepted the Savior through the witness of the church.

Pastor Rick believes that the key to implementing the Great Commission is starting churches. He is convinced that no single church can reach all unchurched people; therefore, he sees the need to parent all kinds of churches to reach all kinds of people with the gospel. Rick is an advocate of starting new churches, reforming existing churches, and challenging existing congregations "to birth new churches for a new generation."[33] He models what he preaches, because Saddleback has sponsored fifteen daughter churches in the thirteen years Rick has been pastor.

Spanish River Church of Boca Raton, Florida. A number of years ago God used Pastor David Nicholas to start what was then Spanish River Presbyterian Church (PCA) in the South Florida community of Boca Raton. Spanish River's missions focus is on planting churches. Ernie Tomforde, lay missions chairman, says, "We recognize that there are all types of outstanding missions opportunities, and we just can't get to all of them."[34]

Initially, the church selected a high-quality person to plant PCA flagship congregations across America that would, in turn, spin off other churches. These now represent some four thousand people in eighteen congregations. Next, Spanish River decided to start churches in other countries as in the States. Today they have established relationships with congregations in fifteen church-planting projects, including such countries as Mexico, India, Chile, Ecuador, Bolivia, Peru, and England.

Church on Brady of Los Angeles, California. Tom Wolf is the pastor of Church on Brady located in Los Angeles. The church has a vision for parenting congregations among various ethnic groups both in the States and in other countries. In recent years, it has started five congregations in Southern California and ten in such countries as Mexico and the Philippines. Their plan is to begin new works in seven different countries within the next year.[35]

Calvary Baptist Church of Erwin, Tennessee. Michael Womack is the pastor of this small, rural, Southern Baptist church located where there are few large churches in the Appalchian Mountains near the border of Tennessee and North Carolina. It has helped to plant one congregation in nearby Johnson City, two in the outlying districts of the county, one in Nashville, one in Maine, one Haitian church in Miami, Florida, one in Indianapolis, Indiana, and two in Europe (Romania). Calvary Baptist demonstrates that the size of a church is not necessarily a factor (as is commonly believed). Small churches can plant new congregations just as effectively as larger churches.

Other excellent churches both large and small have caught a vision to birth churches. The problem in mentioning a few is that you miss so many. Most important, however, is the question: How about your church? What is its attitude toward parenting churches? Could it be included in this list of examples? Is there any reason why it could not be included some time in the future?

Food for Thought

1. Where does the Book of Acts provide examples of planted churches? What was Paul's passion according to Romans 15:20 and 1 Corinthians 3:10? What is your passion?
2. What happens to the growth of the church when it ceases to plant churches? What role does birthing churches play

in the future of the American church? Are you optimistic or pessimistic?

3. Is your church interested or involved in church planting? Why? If not, do some of the reasons in this chapter explain why? Is the church's size a factor? Any reasons not mentioned in the chapter?

4. What is the danger of new churches modeling themselves after the parent church?

5. What are some of the advantages to planting churches under a mother church as opposed to the solo approach? What are the disadvantages?

6. Is your church a part of a denomination or organization? If so, what is its attitude toward starting churches? How might it assist you in this area? If not, would your church benefit by being a part of one of these denominations or organizations? How?

7. Are any of the parent churches mentioned in this chapter located in your area of the country? If so, would you benefit from visiting or corresponding with them?

8. Are there any churches in your area of the country that are planting churches? If so, how might they help you in the same?

7

Renewing Churches

A Fresh Infusion of Life

* Is your church growing, on a plateau, or in decline?
* What do you believe is the future of your church?
* How do you feel about your church undergoing significant change?
* Which is most important to church renewal—the pastor or the process?
* What organizations are available to help churches implement change?

Cherry Hills Community Church is the name painted on a sign out in front of a plain, tired building situated in the older section of a burgeoning bedroom community that neighbors a world-class city in the Southeast. In the early fifties, a popular downtown church planted what was then named Cherry Hills Baptist Church to reach the inhabitants of rural, down-home America. Over the years, the city spread to the country, and large numbers of young, dual-income professionals enveloped the area settling into attractive new homes with fresh, manicured lawns. In spite of all the growth and change, the entrenched churches, most of some denominational stripe, find themselves in desperate decline, gasping for breath. Not Cherry Hills. Within the last ten years it has seen a transformation from a struggling, stagnant collection of inward-focused retirees to an army of excited saints with a passion for reaching the community. In fact, their meetings are not limited to their facility, for they meet in small groups in homes throughout the community where much significant, life-changing ministry takes place. What happened to Cherry Hills Community Church that somehow missed the other area churches? The answer is renewal.

It is true that the future of the American church in the twenty-first century is planting churches. It takes new paradigm churches to reach new generations of Americans who are searching for spiritual truth. But another critical element in a strategy to reach out to America is revitalizing churches. The new generations and the future generations will not search for truth in the numerous typical, traditional churches that mirror the 1950s. Since we now live in the 1990s with the next millennium looking over our shoulders, the American church must not abandon but take advantage of the resources provided by these retiring churches such as their people, property, and facilities that otherwise may be squandered or lost when they close their doors. This will only happen as churches come to grips with their declining situations, cast a fresh vision for renewal, and commit to the renewal process.

However, the pastors and people who make up established churches across America must realize that the terms *renewal* or *revitalization* are less threatening synonyms for the term *change*. Because this nation is living in a momentous and significant period of megachange, the only constant is change itself. If churches expect to survive the 1990s and minister effectively for the Savior in the twenty-first century, they must make some significant changes. So how do churches navigate their way through the sea of swirling change? How can they bridge the gap between the twentieth and the twenty-first centuries? Since so many faltering churches continue to resist change, this chapter will begin with the importance of renewal. Then we will discuss a strategy for renewal and then some models for the same.[1]

The Importance of Renewal

Today numerous voices coming from many different directions are calling out loudly for churches to change or expect the worst. But is this the age-old story of the boy who cried wolf simply repeated for the benefit of the American church at the end of the second millennium?[2] Is there a real wolf lurking in the distance? We will answer this question by examining the church's need for change, its response to that need, and the direction of that change.

The Need for Change

External change. The world outside the church is not simply undergoing change but megachange. America is experiencing change in a way unprecedented in its former history. Presently, some estimate that the knowledge available to man doubles every five to eight years.[3] In *The E-Myth*, Michael Gerber writes, "Today's world is a difficult place. Mankind has experienced more change in the past twenty years than in the 2,000 that preceded them."[4] One trends analyst is "predicting a 'socioquake'—a grass-roots shake-up of society prompted by more change in the next 10 years than in the last 90."[5] In *Future Shock*, a book written in 1970 to examine the process of change, Alvin Toffler argued that the acceleration of change would transform society, and he was correct.[6] Later he wrote a third work, *Power Shift*, which he says is "the culmination of a twenty-five year effort to make sense of the astonishing changes propelling us into the 21st century."[7]

The change over the past few years has left no rock unturned. It has affected the social, economic, political, religious, and technological arenas of life all around us. It has seen the shift of power and influence from the Pre-Boomer Generation to the vastly different Baby Boom and Baby Bust Generations. It has witnessed the descent from a churched, theistic culture in the late 1940s and 1950s to a secular, naturalistic culture in the 1990s. Joel Barker writes about the profound impact of all this change: "In the last twenty years, all of western society has been through extraordinary turbulent times. We have been living in a time when fundamental rules, the basic ways we do things, have been altered dramatically. . . . These kinds of dramatic changes are extremely important because they have created in us a special sense of impermanence which generates tremendous discomfort."[8]

Internal change. The now fragile world of the American church is also undergoing significant change. Much of this was demonstrated in chapter 3. There we discovered that a significant number of the churches in the nation are on a plateau or in decline. Those that are growing are doing so primarily as the result of transfer growth (the reshuffling of the saints) and biological growth, not conversion growth. Perhaps the current denominational situation can be summed up best by Kirk Hadaway, a church-growth research specialist with the Southern Baptist Convention, who writes: "The typical church in almost any American denomination is either on a plateau or declining in membership and participation. Rapid growth is atypical, and among older congregations the pattern is even more pronounced and declines are the rule; growth is the rare exception."[9]

Lyle Schaller asks: "What is one of the most common characteristics of a congregation that is experiencing a gradual decrease in numbers? . . . During the past decade the average attendance in Sunday school is down 25 percent, worship attendance has dropped by 20 percent, after adjusting for inflation, member contributions are down 15 percent, and the high school youth group has 35 percent fewer teenagers involved on a regular basis."[10]

Most who address this situation point out that while the mainline denominations are in steep decline, conservative churches are on an incline. However, it is important for evangelicals to know that all kinds of religious groups are often placed under the label "conservative." Some examples are the Jehovah's Witnesses (121 percent), the Mormons (116 percent), the Seventh-Day Adventists (79 percent), and the Roman Catholics, who are showing some growth due to Hispanic immigration in the South. Some churches like the Southern Baptists are showing slight if any growth, and this is due to their heavy emphasis on church planting. Churches experiencing astounding growth are the Church of God (Cleveland: 147 percent), the Assemblies of God (116 percent), and the Church of the Nazarene (50 percent), who have also placed heavy stress on church planting.[11]

As America experiences momentous change, so must its churches change in their attempts to communicate and implement the Good News of Jesus Christ. The cultural leap from the vast secular world populated by unchurched people to the cultural values and styles of the typical church is too great. Unlike the past decades, the church must no longer remain comfortably situated behind its walls waiting for the community to come to it; rather, it must go to its community. In the process, it will have to adapt to, not accommodate, that community's culture.

The Response to Change

Should it change? In light of the present declining condition of the church, the need for change seems obvious. Callahan writes, "The loss and the decline should be teaching us something. The ways in which we have been doing leadership are no longer working on this mission field on which we now find ourselves. In a clear sense, I think this is God's way of teaching us that what we have been doing no longer works. Ultimately, we will continue to lose members until we finally figure that out."[12]

But what does the Bible say about change? Should the church change at all? Is the solution found in changing what the typical church believes (its doctrine) or how it practices what it believes (its programs) or neither? In the 1960s, many of the old-line denominational churches stopped planting congregations and changed their theology while maintaining their old methodology. The result was disastrous. The question is, How should the church today respond biblically to change?

A biblical theology of change centers on understanding the differences between the functions of the church and the forms those functions take in its ministry. On the one hand, the functions are biblical, eternal truths of Scripture that are binding on the church regardless the era. They answer the question, *What* is the church supposed to do? They consist of such truths as evangelism, teaching, prayer, discipleship, leadership, equipping, and worship that never change.

On the other hand, the forms of ministry direct *how* and *when* the church does *what* it does. They are not binding on the church and represent that aspect of the church that legitimately changes in order to minister most effectively to its culture. They are the forms that the functions take in each era.

Some examples will help. Evangelism is a ministry function that must always characterize the church. The forms that it takes, however, may vary according to the church's present culture. The form could be one or a combination of pastoral, revival, visitation, educational, mass-media, or fellowship evangelism. Another example is worship. Essentially, worship is a function of the church that may take a contemporary or traditional form or both depending on what the terms *contemporary* and *traditional* mean in any given era.

Scripture grants the church much freedom for the forms its ministries take. In 1 Corinthians 9:19–23, Paul writes that he has certain rights as a Christian. However, he was willing to forgo them if it meant reaching his generation for the Savior. In doing so, he does not, however, advocate disobedience to biblical imperatives. When the Bible permitted it, Paul was willing to adapt to the culture, whether under the law or not, to win people for Christ.

Can it change? The question is, Can struggling, established churches be revitalized? The reason for the question is that some do not believe this is possible. For example, Ralph Neighbour, Jr., after working with twenty-one pastors, concludes that they cannot. He writes, "Our Lord told us over 2,000 years ago *it could not be done.* Every time we try to ignore His clear teaching, we fail. In retrospect, I could have saved myself 24 years of dreaming an impossible dream if I had taken His admonition literally."[13] Writing in 1972, Lyle Schaller warns: "Anyone seriously interested in planned social change would be well advised to recognize two facts of life. First, despite the claims of many, relatively little is known about how to achieve predictable change. Second, much of what is known will not work."[14]

George Barna is more positive. In his discussion of the options of church planting versus church revitalization, he comments:

> When I speak to groups of pastors about this information, they often ask about the difference between planting a new church and renewing an existing church using these perspectives and techniques. The fact is that it is substantially easier to start fresh than to recast an existing body into a new entity.
>
> There are, however, examples of churches in which a stagnant body has had new life breathed into it through a change of direction or nature.[15]

All three positions present elements of truth that serve to wave a red warning flag that signals the difficulties of church renewal. Neighbour and Schaller warn of the difficulties and heartache that have resulted in a ministry terrain strewn with casualties. Anyone who attempts to revitalize churches must proceed cautiously with eyes open.

Ralph Neighbour's experience has proved to be more negative than that of others, and much printer's ink has been spilled to provide more information on the topic of change since Schaller wrote *The Change Agent* in 1972. Barna indicates that planting churches is easier than renewing them. Actually, both church planting and church renewal have their individual problems. The question is, Which set of problems are you most comfortable with?

Barna is correct when he says that churches exist which have experienced successful renewal. Actually, they are numerous, and my prayer is, "May their tribe increase." One notable example is Woodale Church in Eden Prairie, Minnesota, which over the past fifteen years has experienced a process of renewal and growth that has placed it on the cutting edge in reaching out to the lost and in meeting the spiritual needs of its people. Another example is Bear Valley Baptist Church in Denver, Colorado, which has exerted an impact on the city through its many ministries. Other notable examples exist as well. In fact, in the Dallas-Fort Worth metroplex, I am aware of several outstanding examples. More will be said about some of these churches later in the chapter.

Must it change? My response is that churches that desire to implement Christ's mission have no choice. Lyle Schaller is one of America's foremost church consultants with more than thirty years of experience. He writes:

> From a different perspective, another question can be asked. What is the number-one issue facing Christian organizations on the North American continent today? What is the one issue that faces every congregation, denomination, movement, theological seminary, parachurch organization, interchurch agency? Dwindling numbers? Money? Social justice? Com-

petent leadership? The growing dysfunctional nature of ecclesiastical structures? Television? The new immigration from the Pacific Rim and Latin America? Governmental regulations? Human sexuality? The fact our society has become an increasingly barren and hostile environment for rearing children? The shift from verbal to visual communication?

After more than three decades spent working with thousands of congregational, denominational, seminary, and parachurch leaders from more than five dozen traditions, this observer places a one-sentence issue at the top of that list. *The need to initiate and implement planned change from within an organization.* That is the number-one issue today for most congregations, denominations, theological seminaries, parachurch organizations, and reform movements.[16]

The Direction of Change

Wrapped up in the very essence of change is the idea of movement. Change is dynamic, not static. And wrapped up in the essence of movement is destination. The question is, Where will this change take renewed churches? What will they look like at the end of the process?

A number of traditional churches in the last few years have come to a place where they realize that they must change to survive. The problem is they believe that survival means maintaining the status quo or worse a return to days gone by. Common are the words, "We're simply not working hard enough at what we're doing—we need more commitment," or "We need to return to the good ol' days when this church was full of dedicated people." This is a formula for disaster.

There are two truths that must be remembered in terms of the direction of revitalization. First, in light of today's accelerating megachange, every church must look to the future. Many churches desire to return to the past—to church life as it was in the 1950s when America was largely a churched culture. The problem is that the culture in the 1990s is secular, post-Christian. To minister in a post-

Christian culture as if it were a churched culture is ecclesiastical suicide. Some are not talking about returning to the 1950s but to a particular time in the past when their church was thriving. Regardless, the world today and tomorrow will always be different from the past. To return to any past era for ministry will confine the church's ministry to the people of that era.

A second truth is that the people of today and tomorrow are different from those of yesterday. In chapter 2, I discussed the three basic generations: Pre-Boomers, Baby Boomers, and Baby Busters. The idea of returning to a past ministry is to minister to a distinct generation, the Pre-Boomers. While there is nothing wrong with ministering to this generation, it does miss the other two. The real problem is that the future of America is the Baby Boomers and the Baby Busters. Churches that minister solely to the Pre-Boom Generation will have to use forms (the grand old hymns, one-hour sermons, King James prayers, formal attire, and so on) that appeal to these people but turn off the other generations. Again, this is one of the reasons so many left the churches in the 1960s and 1970s. The church that plans to serve Christ in the future must minister to those who will be a part of the future as well as the past.

Churches that desire to impact future generations for the Savior must think in terms of new paradigms. They must ask such critical questions as, What forms will ministry need to take in the twenty-first century to most effectively minister God's truth to the people of the twenty-first century and beyond? Is the Sunday school the answer, or should we transition to small-group ministries exclusively? Are there other ways to communicate God's truth in addition to the sermon—could a church also hold a debate or a round-table discussion? Could it use the mini-drama and video clips in the service? Kennon Callahan writes, "New understandings of doing ministry must be created with each new generation for the church's mission to move forward. When an older generation imposes its understanding on the new generation—however innocently—both groupings become dysfunctional. Each new generation must carve out an understanding of ministry that matches its times."[17]

To illustrate this point, consider the church that is becoming the best-known and largest in America—Willow Creek Community Church near Chicago, Illinois. Currently, it is considered to be on the cutting edge in terms of significant, effective ministry. Yet, if it plans to minister to the generations of the twenty-first century, it will need to ask and answer these same types of questions. I would predict that their present ministry format will be considered traditional within five to ten years. Willow Creek is aware of all this, however, and has adopted a dynamic approach to stay current—it is not the same church it was in the 1980s. Churches that refuse to adapt will not make it into the next millennium; people will simply go elsewhere.

Another area that needs much thought is the role of the laity in ministry and that of women in particular. The typical small church across America hires a pastor to do the work of the ministry, whereas, Scripture clearly indicates that every member is a minister (Eph. 4:11). It is essential to the future of the American church that the scriptural view gain preeminence. Not only is more lay participation needed in the church, but involvement of laypeople in evangelism in the marketplace is critical if the church is to have impact on a generation that no longer frequents the local church. The church must also determine not so much what women cannot do in terms of ministry, but what they can do. Many Christian women sense God's direction to be evangelists, teachers, and leaders and have much to offer the church, yet they are limited in their ministries by non-biblical traditions. This needs careful attention and change if the Church of Jesus Christ is to be all that it can be in the twenty-first century.

All this is not to argue that classical churches should make massive changes immediately. That, too, would mean certain death. Churches that are rapidly declining will have to make major changes over a short period of time, but they find themselves caught in the horns of a dilemma. Not to pursue change insures certain death; however, the kinds of changes necessary for renewal may be so massive that they, too, mean death. The point is that all churches need to constantly evaluate their ministry forms and implement incremental changes wherever the church is located on the ministry spectrum from traditional to contemporary.

A Strategy for Renewal

Once the American church has grasped the importance of revitalizing its plateaued and dying churches, next it must develop a strategy for accomplishing renewal. The following strategy will emphasize the leadership and context for renewal and then conclude with a process for the same.

The Leadership for Renewal

As the leadership of an organization goes, so goes that organization. This maxim applies strongly to churches, especially in light of their voluntary status. It is rare that a church is planted or revitalized without the consent and full backing of the pastor. Peter Wagner emphasizes the importance of the pastor to the ministry of the church when he writes: "In America, the primary catalytic factor for growth in a local church is the pastor."[18] Here we must ask a critical question, What kind of leaders are good at leading churches through renewal?

Before answering this question, however, I must deal with an important concept that I call the "leadership fallacy." Popular wisdom in the U.S. today communicates that a person can be anything he or she wants to be; it is a part of the American Dream. This concept has also subtly slipped into the thinking of the Christian community as well and has left its fingerprints all over the concept of pastoral leadership. For example, the average person who has decided to go into pastoral ministry today assumes that he is a leader who can competently lead any church regardless of its condition. The biblical truth is that each Christian is unique, and some who assume the role of pastor are better at leading churches than others. Different people have different leadership styles. Schaller writes: "These differences have also made obsolete the old cliché, 'Every minister should be able to serve any congregation.'"[19]

The biblical truth is that each person comes into this world as an image bearer with a unique design from the sovereign Creator (see Ps. 19:1; 119:73; 139:13–14; Jer. 1:5).[20] While Christians may have similar designs, no two are the same. Paul demonstrates this in his analogy between believers who make up the church, the body of Christ, and the human body: "If the whole body were an eye, where would the sense of hearing be? If the whole body were an ear, where would the sense of smell be? But in fact God has arranged the parts in the body, every one of them, just as he wanted them to be. If they were all one part, where would the body be? As it is, there are many parts, but one body" (1 Cor. 12:17–20).

The fact that God has sovereignly designed each Christian differently emphasizes the truth that they cannot serve God in whatever manner they please. One of Paul's points in 1 Corinthians 12 is that an eye cannot serve God effectively as an ear nor an ear as an eye. Therefore, those who aspire to and those already in Christian ministry must take into account their divine designs. Failure to discern one's design most often results either in ministry burnout, which could lead to ministry dropout, or in a lifetime of ineffective ministry.

The point in this discussion is that some are going to be better at certain aspects of leadership than others. God has designed some people to lead in birthing churches. He has designed others to lead in an interim ministry. He has designed still others as change agents to lead churches through renewal.

Having examined the leadership fallacy, we are ready to answer the question, What kinds of leaders are good at taking their churches through revitalization? The answer is that leaders' particular ministries are based on their spiritual gifts, driven by their passion, poured through their personalities, authenticated by their spiritual character, and enhanced by their natural abilities.

Spiritual gifts. God has bestowed on all his children various spiritual gifts (see 1 Cor. 12:7–11; Eph. 4:7). But certain gifts are common to revitalization pastors:

1. *Leadership* (see Rom. 12:8). This gift characterizes those with a clear, focused vision who articulate that vision in a way that influences others to become followers. It takes pastors with the gift of leadership to move churches off plateaus or turn around those in decline.
2. *Faith* (see 1 Cor. 12:9). This gift is the ability to envision what needs to be done and to trust God to accomplish it in spite of overwhelming obstacles. It helps pastors want to revitalize their churches and to believe that change is possible.
3. *Exhortation* (see Rom. 12:8). This is the ability to encourage and console when necessary while confronting and admonishing others. Plateaued and dying churches are in need of constant, daily encouragement and consolation balanced with a healthy amount of confrontation and admonition to move toward renewal.
4. *Preaching.* It appears to be one of the spiritual gifts because of its association with the gift of being an apostle and teacher (see 1 Tim. 2:7; 2 Tim. 1:11). Preaching is the ability to relevantly and persuasively communicate God's Word with clarity and power so as to impact people's

lives. This is vital in the leader's role as vision caster as well as the communicator of biblical truth.

5. *Evangelism* (see Eph. 4:11). This is the ability to communicate clearly Christ's gospel to unbelievers individually or corporately so that they accept him. One of the reasons why a church is on a plateau or is in decline is because it has focused on inreach as opposed to outreach. A leader with the gift of evangelism can prove infectious around these kinds of churches.

Does church revitalization require all of these gifts? No, but wisdom dictates that the more the better—leaders with more of these gifts will function better as change agents.

Passion. God's children are also designed with a unique passion. Passion is a feeling that some have described as a burning, gut feeling that a particular ministry is where God wants you to be. In Romans 15:20, Paul uses the term *ambition* to communicate his passion to proclaim the gospel to the Gentiles (see Rom. 15:16). It serves to focus and motivate the believer's spiritual gifts. Leaders who are renewal agents have a passion for people in plateaued or declining situations. They feel much like the Savior who, "when he saw the crowds, he had compassion on them, because they were harassed and helpless, like sheep without a shepherd" (Matt. 9:36). They are convinced that in these situations they can make a difference.

Temperament. In addition to their spiritual gifts and passion, each in God's family has a unique personality or temperament. As with a leader's gifts and passion, so change agents have a certain temperament that supplies unique personal character strengths for a revitalization ministry.

A tool that has proved most helpful in discovering one's temperament is the *Personal Profile* (or the *Biblical Personal Profile*).[21] In his doctoral dissertation, Robert Thomas used the *Biblical Personal Profile* to discover the specific personality characteristics of effective renewal pastors. He found that they fell within the persuader pattern. This pattern is the result of bringing together what the *Profile* calls a High I temperament with a secondary, supporting D temperament. A biblical example of one with the persuader pattern is Peter. The following is a description of the pattern:

> Persuaders work with and through people. That is, they strive to do business in a friendly way while pushing forward to win their own objectives. Possessing an outgoing interest in people, Persuaders have the ability to gain the respect and confidence of various types of individuals. This ability is particularly helpful to Persuaders in winning positions of authority. In addition, they seek work assignments which provide opportunities to make them look good. Work with people, challenging assignments, variety of work and activities which require mobility provide the most favorable environment for Persuaders. However, they may be too optimistic about the results of projects and the potential of people. Persuaders also tend to overestimate their ability to change the behavior of others. While Persuaders seek freedom from routine and regimentation, they do need to be supplied with analytical data on a systematic basis. When they are alerted to the importance of "little things," adequate information helps them to control impulsiveness.[22]

This profile serves as a starting place for discovering leaders who are designed for church renewal. The farther one moves from this point in temperament, the less likely they will function well in leading churches through revitalization.[23]

While not a part of his or her divine design, the leader's spiritual character authenticates his or her ministry. God may have designed a person for a ministry of renewal; however, if that person does not demonstrate spiritual character, he or she does not have the spiritual qualifications for any kind of ministry. On the one hand, to a certain extent, the ability to lead in renewal comes from God regardless of the individual.

On the other, godliness is not automatic—it must be pursued daily. Paul encourages the leader to "train yourself to be godly" (1 Tim. 4:7).

Spiritual qualifications. What are the spiritual qualifications for leadership? Paul lists them in 1 Timothy 3:1–7 and Titus 1:6–9. Those desiring positions of leadership in general and church renewal in particular would be wise to review these qualifications regularly. 1 Timothy 3:2 says: "Now the overseer must be above reproach." If one does not meet the qualifications for leadership in some way, then he must not pursue a ministry of revitalization. Instead, with God's help he should do everything possible to correct any discrepancies first. If one in a position of leadership finds that he no longer meets these qualifications, he must either take a leave of absence to correct the inadequacies or resign. Failure to do so has the potential to destroy the ministry as demonstrated by far too many pastors and televangelists in the 1980s and 1990s.

Leading healthy churches as a pastor has proved difficult in the last few decades. Attempting to lead dysfunctional congregations through renewal is even more difficult. Those who dare to lead them in the point position must be people of integrity. Those both inside and outside the church will examine and question their character. Only pastors who demonstrate Christlikeness will survive.

Talents. Finally, what kinds of natural abilities and talents enhance the ministry of renewal? The answer is found in examining the life of a biblical change agent—Nehemiah—who was used by God to lead the Jews in postexilic Jerusalem through renewal. Renewal agents seldom have all these abilities as Nehemiah did, but they should identify with a sufficient number of them. I associate some of these abilities with leadership, others with administration.

On the *leadership* side of the ledger, talented change agents are often catalysts, outsiders, problem-solvers, visionaries, motivators, persuaders, risk takers, empathizers, and perseverers. Nehemiah was a *catalyst* as he bravely took the initiative to speak with King Artaxerxes about the dreadful circumstances in Jerusalem (see Neh. 2:1–3), and he initiated contact with the Jews in Jerusalem (see Neh. 2:11). In *Discovering the Future*, Barker writes: "The paradigm shifter is a catalyst, a change agent, and part of the role of a catalyst is to stir things up."[24]

Nehemiah was an *outsider*. Initially, Nehemiah lived not in Jerusalem but Susa, about 250 miles east of Babylon (see Neh. 1:1). Thus he was able to bring fresh perspective from a different paradigm to a situation immersed in a painful, discouraging status quo. Barker asks: "What kind of person is a paradigm shifter? . . . The short answer is simple: an outsider."[25] This should be most encouraging to new pastors. However, it does not mean that insiders cannot be effective change agents as well.

Nehemiah was a *problem-solver*. Everywhere he looked, he saw problems. Jerusalem was in disarray, the walls were broken down, and the gates were burned to the ground. The people were emotionally stressed out and shamed (see Neh. 1:3), but he viewed the problems as a challenge and was able to lead them in solving their problems.

Nehemiah was a *visionary*. He carried a snapshot of the rebuilt walls and gates of Jerusalem in his mental wallet until the vision was realized (see Neh. 2:17). Renewal agents have the innate ability to see what nonvisionaries cannot see. They see in their heads the exciting future of the churches they hunger to revitalize.

Nehemiah was a *motivator*. He catalyzed the Jews to rebuild Jerusalem's walls (see Neh. 2:17–18). Change agents will find that motivation in ministry is a never-ending process. Once people accomplish their vision, the tendency is to sit back and rest on their laurels.

Nehemiah was a *persuader*. God used Nehemiah to persuade a pagan king to his cause (see Neh. 2:5–8). This was based not on manipulation but on Nehemiah's godly example. The discussion above on temperament revealed that the persuader pattern best characterized pastors whom God has used to revitalize churches.

Nehemiah was a *risk-taker*. He risked his life when he appeared before the king with a sad countenance (see Neh. 2:1–2; Esther 4:11). He risked his leadership reputation when he challenged the Jews to rebuild the city walls (see Neh. 2:16–17). Barker writes: "Non-rational decision-making and courage; those are the two hallmarks of a leader. And can you think of any place where leadership is required more than the changing of paradigms? Leaders are willing to take a risk."[26]

Nehemiah was an *empathizer*. He expressed empathy and compassion for the Jews and their plight in Jerusalem. He spent several days weeping, fasting, and mourning because he cared about them (see Neh. 1:4). Task-oriented change agents can accomplish their goals of renewal but often run over people in the process. They must be balanced with empathy for people.

Finally, Nehemiah was a *perseverer*. He "hung tough" in spite of tremendous odds. This is demonstrated in Nehemiah 4:1–6:14 where he responded to those who would benefit if he resigned from his mission. The temptation to quit constantly beckons to those who would lead churches in the renewal process. Vision vampires are ready to pounce and suck the lifeblood out of the dream. This does not mean that a leader should never give up on a church. Some churches need to hear the last rites. It does mean that they should not be too quick to quit.

On the *administrative* side, revitalizers are planners, recruiters, organizers, and good delegators. Nehemiah was a *planner*. When he spoke to King Artaxerxes, he obviously had a plan in his head if not in his hand (see Neh. 2:6–8). Also, the rebuilding of the walls necessitated a plan (see Neh. 3). Most struggling churches expect the renewal agent to arrive with a plan. The plan is vital to accomplishing the mission and vision.

Nehemiah was a *recruiter*. It appears that Nehemiah was able to recruit most if not all the Jews to implement his plan in spite of their depressed condition (see Neh. 2:17–20). In order to implement a dream, leaders must be able to win allies to be a part of the team if they are to realize the dream.

Nehemiah was an *organizer*. He displayed his talent for organization as the Jews initiated the building project. Some were assigned one project, while others worked on another (see Neh. 3:1, 3). Revitalizers need to be able to organize different areas such as finances, people, and equipment if they are to accomplish the dream. Otherwise, the result is ministry chaos.

Finally, Nehemiah was a *delegator*. The truth is that he did not rebuild the walls of Jerusalem, nor did he attempt to. He delegated this responsibility to other people, many of whom are named in chapter 3. Like an athletic coach, revitalizers must not attempt to play every position on the team but encourage and allow others to play their positions accordingly.

The Context for Renewal

Having answered the question, What kind of leaders make good revitalizers?, the next question asks, What kind of environment facilitates renewal? The answer is a church context that displays at least some of the following characteristics.

The church that facilitates renewal follows biblical principles. A question that is important to all Christians who desire to serve the Savior is, How can I know the will of God? In *Decision Making and the Will of God*, Gary Friesen demonstrates that the Christian community is divided on the answer to this question.[27] However, all agree that aspects of the will of God are found in the Word of God, the Bible. While the culture will change, the Scripture remains constant and is the Christian's norm for church life, governing both church planting and church renewal. In the Bible, God has provided for his church various biblical principles vital to renewal.

1. Scripture indicates that the purpose of the church is to glorify God (see Ps. 22:23; Rom. 15:6).[28] This answers the question of why the church is here on the earth.
2. The mission of the church, covered in chapter 5, is the Great Commission—Matthew 28:19–20 and Mark 16:15. It concerns what the church is supposed to be doing here on the earth.
3. The New Testament presents various functions that are to be carried out by Christ's church, such as those found in Acts 2:42–47: teaching, giving, prayer, fellowship, and worship.
4. Christ instituted the ordinances of baptism (see Acts 2:38; 10:47–48) and the Lord's supper (see Matt. 26:26–30; 1 Cor. 11:23–26) to be remembered and celebrated by his church.
5. God has ordained that spiritually qualified elders and deacons (see 1 Tim. 3:1–13) provide leadership for the church.
6. He has also provided each person in the church with spiritual gifts (see 1 Cor. 12:7–11) to serve the church and accomplish its ministry.

The church that facilitates renewal allows its professional leadership team to lead. Lyle Schaller writes: "Popular wisdom today insists that everyone has a right to participate in the making of any decision that will affect one's future in a significant way."[29] Thus, congregations prefer congregational rule because it allows them to have their say. Many laymen prefer to sit on boards where the pastor is "just another one of the boys" (one vote) or has no vote at all. This is the board-run church. Some justify this by citing passages that refer to the priesthood of all believers.

However, a number of problems exist with this approach. First, the average layperson who loves Christ does not have the time nor the training to make major leadership decisions affecting the life of the church. It is the pastor (and in large churches the pastoral team) who spends more than fifty hours a week leading and equipping the flock. Because he is immersed in the day-to-day ministry of the church, he has his finger on the pulse of the congregation. Also, some decisions have to be made quickly, as those in the marketplace have learned. From the perspective of the economy of time, a board-run church is a cumbersome thing. Any delay could cost the church in a number of ways including dollars and cents as well as ministry advantage. In addition, some lay leaders do not have leadership gifts or abilities and know little about leadership. While others lead in a business or some other nonvoluntary setting, it is the pastor who is supposedly trained to lead a voluntary organization such as the church.[30]

Second, when the pastor brings a good proposal to many lay boards, it is talked to death and thus dies in the process. Certain well-intentioned members have strong opinions, and the proposal is compromised to the point that it no longer bears any resemblance to the original. It loses all its potency; it reduces to the least common denominator. Schaller writes that "participatory democracy and planned change are incompatible . . . participatory democracy tends to reinforce the status quo."[31] Participatory democracy is characteristic of small churches and could have something to do with why so many stay small. A large church could never function this way.[32]

Schaller writes that healthy growing churches are characterized by strong pastoral leadership.[33] Churches that are on a plateau or are in decline need strong leadership if renewal is to happen. An aspect of renewal is church growth. The typical church board is a standing committee. Schaller states that standing committees by nature prefer the status quo.[34] The kind of committee that promotes change is the ad hoc committee that disbands after it completes its assignment.

Finally, the doctrine of the priesthood of all believers is the truth that all Christians are to serve Christ. This does not mean, however, that laypeople must sit on church boards and tell the pastor how to run the church. Scripture does not teach this, in fact, it teaches otherwise.[35] The church that insists on a lay board would be much more effective if a qualified pastor served as the leader of the leaders. A better option is for qualified lay leaders to serve not on the board but as leaders of key ministries in the church.

The church that facilitates revitalization has a high level of trust. In healthy growing churches, the people trust their leadership. In church planting, people in the core group grant this trust to the pastor until he proves otherwise. In church renewal, the pastor has to earn this trust. Several ingredients lead to the creation of an atmosphere of trust in a congregation. First is the leadership's character. Godly character is foundational to any leadership (see 1 Tim. 3:1–13, Tit. 1:6–9). It is the essential element that qualifies Christians to lead others. Not only does it earn people's respect, but most important, it produces trust—the most essential factor in relationships. The leadership must be trusted to be followed.

A second ingredient is competence. The people must believe that the leadership both knows how to lead and, in fact, can lead. Good leaders are learners; consequently, competent leaders carve out time in their busy schedules to read, attend seminars, and expand their world. They also demonstrate their leadership ability in the trenches. This does not mean that they do not take risks and make some mistakes. Again, good leaders are learners. The question is, Do they learn from their mistakes?

A third ingredient that leads to trust is the belief that the leadership has the best interests of the congregation at heart. In short, people want their pastor to love them (see 1 Tim. 4:12; 6:11). A person's leadership style can potentially locate at one of two extremes—a strong task orientation or a strong people orientation. One of the problems of a strong task-oriented leadership style mentioned earlier is that people feel run over. While this leader may truly have the congregation's best interests at heart, he becomes so intent on accomplishing his mission that he fails to communicate his care and concern for the people he seeks to lead. Consequently, these leaders must pay regular attention to their people skills if they are to develop trust in the congregation.

The church that encourages renewal communicates well. Good communication is critical to church renewal regardless of where the church is in the process. Normal people want to know what is happening or else they feel suspicious. When the church communicates well, people feel trusted and are willing to return that trust.

The problem is that declining churches do not communicate well if at all. Consequently, the church must work hard at establishing good lines of communication. This is accomplished in several ways:

1. Perhaps most important, be a good listener. Schaller writes that "active listening is one of the most important components for effecting a strategy of planned change within any organization."[36] In fact, most people are willing to go along with change as long as they believe they are heard, even if the church does not take their advice.
2. Take advantage of every opportunity to communicate the church's vision and mission for renewal and how it plans to implement them. Gary McIntosh advises "Give people specifics. Explain how each person, class or group can contribute to the turnaround. Keep people informed by writing letters to their home. Use small group meetings or desserts where people may hear what steps are being taken for the future and have opportunity to ask questions. Make public all that is appropriate. Maintain a spirit of openness and vulnerability."[37]

3. Pay special attention to any misinformation. When leaders come across misinformation, they must act quickly. This involves tracking down the original source and correcting the bad information. If the source is motivated by malice, then he or she should be disciplined (see Matt. 18:15–19).
4. Communicate through progress reports. It is not a good idea to surprise people. Let them know in advance of potential changes. This gives them time to think about those changes and talk themselves into acceptance.
5. Leak accurate information to the congregation. Let the proverbial cat out of the bag during informal conversations. This, too, gives people the time that they need to reach a point of acceptance.
6. Good communication is positive communication. Positive people motivate while negative people discourage. Emphasize the advantages of the potential changes. Find the plus in every change no matter how painful it may be.

The environment that facilitates renewal understands why people resist change. One reason is felt needs—people may resist change because they do not feel a need to change. If you asked them to produce a list of their felt needs, change would not be among them. This is because some are not aware that the church is hopelessly immersed in the status quo; they believe that all is well. Others are not aware of all the change that is taking place in the world around them. Somehow they have effectively isolated and insulated themselves from it. They remain in their own private world ignoring the public world.

Another reason people resist change is that most people prefer the status quo. They are comparable to the infant who prefers the comfort and safety of its mother's womb rather than a birth into a world of much pain and discomfort. A key issue is control. To move out of your comfort zone is to risk loss of control over yourself and your environment. Why would anyone want to risk that?

A third reason is the congregation's values. Every church has a philosophy of ministry that consists of its core values, and what people value in their church is of great importance to them. In fact, people are sometimes willing to give their lives for their values, such as the men and women who have given their lives in battle for their country. While church people may not give their lives for their congregational values, they will be quick to fight over them.

People may also resist change because of vested interests. Over a period of time in every church, various benefits accrue to certain people such as position, power, and prestige. Change threatens these benefits. For example, if a man has gained a position of power and prestige through many years on the church board, he will be quick to protect his best interests if they are threatened by change.

The stress of change is also an important factor. Much change has taken place in the 1980s, and it is only accelerating in the 1990s. All evidence indicates that the pace will increase in the early twenty-first century. The problem for churched people is change overload. People can only handle so much change over a short period of time. Alvin Toffler warns that to subject people to too much change over a brief time span results in future shock or shattering stress and disorientation.

Change may be slowed by sacred cows. In *Say No, Say Yes to Change*, Elaine Dickson writes: "We give things a sacred quality although they are not intrinsically sacred. Some things become our 'sacred cows.' Whatever is considered sacred—genuine or not—becomes relatively immune to change.'"[38] National examples are the "Star Spangled Banner" and the American flag. Consider the uproar when certain celebrities have sung a different rendition of the national anthem, or when protestors have burned the flag. Over the years, congregations have grazed sacred cows on the front lawn of the church. Some examples are the old hymns of the faith, the King James Bible, King James style prayers, formal attire, and three meetings a week. In people's minds these "cows" become sacrosanct. To discontinue any of them is tantamount to ripping the Book of Romans out of the Bible.

A final reason people resist change is self-centeredness. Most discussions about why people refuse to change seldom mention self-centeredness, especially when the people themselves are involved in that discussion. Reality is that most of us at some time put ourselves and our best interests first. This becomes evident in a meet-my-needs mentality and the need people have to be in control of their circumstances. The ultimate source of this is the flesh or sinful nature (see Gal. 5:16–17).[39]

The church that establishes a good context for revitalization understands who votes for and against change. The people who make up the church in general and the leadership board in particular fall within certain categories in terms of their openness to change. One category is the early adopters. They are the 2 to 18 percent of the congregation who have grown tired of the status quo and are open to change and new ideas. Many are innovators and pioneers in terms of new ideas. They often tend to be the younger members who are well educated and have been exposed to lots of change in other contexts. An important principle of revitalization is to recruit them as active allies for the program of change.

Another category is the never adopters. Of the four categories of change response, they are the people who are opposite of the early adopters—they refuse to vote in favor of change. They are the church's guardians of the status quo. An extreme example is the deacon who walks in late to a board meeting and realizes that a vote is being taken and responds, "I don't know what you're voting on, but whatever it is I'm against it." Often they are the squeaky wheels of the church who attract attention far out of proportion to their numbers.

The problem is that most boards give in to their demands in the name of congregational unity, and this vocal minority controls the silent majority. If the vote does not go their way, often they will exit the church. An important principle of renewal is not to give in to these kinds of people. If they threaten to leave, let them leave.

A third category is the middle adopters. They are located between the two extremes—the early adopters and the never adopters. They are clearly the majority in most churches and make up 60 to 80 percent of the congregation. Their tendency is to vote for the status quo. They do not actively pursue change unless given good reasons for it. In the renewal process, they are the key group, because in light of their sheer numbers, their response to change will determine whether or not revitalization takes place. A key to renewal is to communicate with them and provide them with all the good reasons for change.

A final category is the late adopters. They are located between the middle adopters and the never adopters. They are the last in the church to accept a new idea or program of change. They usually wait until they can discern how the winds of change are blowing in the congregation as a whole. If the congregation is for change, eventually they are for change. If the congregation is opposed to change, they will oppose it as well. The renewal principle for these people is to be patient with them. If the congregation votes for change, in time they will come around.

Some Models for Church Renewal

Who is involved in revitalizing churches across America? Remarkably, not a lot of activity is taking place in proportion to the number of churches that are struggling, especially on the denominational level. However, a number of organizations have come into existence that are operating at other levels and are helping churches accomplish renewal and growth.

Denominational Organizations

A handful of organizations at a denominational level have begun to address the areas of church revitalization and growth. We will look briefly at five.

The Southern Baptist Convention. Early in 1990 Dr. Harry Piland pioneered the initial vision that has led to the development of the Southern Baptist program for renewal called Great Commission Breakthrough. It is a church process that uses a Great Commission Breakthrough consultant to work with a local pastor through the Sunday school and other church organizations to accomplish the Great Commission mandate.

The entire project was initiated in 1990 with the creation of a Great Commission Breakthrough Task Force. Their goal was to turn a vision into a reality. Between October 1990 and September 1991, five hundred consultants volunteered and were trained. This led to Great Commission Breakthrough consultations in 358 pilot churches, which reported an average increase of twenty-seven in Sunday school enrollment in a year when the average increase in the SBC was 4.5 per church.[40]

The current goal is to train seven thousand consultants by September 1995 to conduct the Great Commission Breakthrough in fourteen thousand churches. The long-range goal from 1995 to 2000 is to train another eight thousand consultants, creating the potential to conduct the Great Commission Breakthrough in more than thirty thousand churches.

Prior to Great Commission Breakthrough, however, other pastors have had a positive impact on dying congregations in the Southern Baptist Convention. Two of the most innovative have been Dr. Charles Stanley, the pastor of First Baptist

179

Church of Atlanta, Georgia, and Dr. Ed Young, the pastor of Second Baptist Church in Houston, Texas.

The United Methodist Church. With sagging attendance, the United Methodists have taken steps to initiate renewal in their churches. The United Methodist General Board of Discipleship has created Vision 2000, a project centered on training local church teams to initiate change in worship styles and congregational techniques to attract new people. Those who participate in Vision 2000 training sessions attend workshops on subjects ranging from how to revamp Sunday school to how to incorporate different music designed to revive uninspired worship. Vision 2000 seminars may also focus on reaching out to Hispanics, Baby Boomers, singles, and older adults.[41]

The Evangelical Free Church of America. Under the leadership of Paul Cedar, the Evangelical Free Church is one of the premier organizations that has taken a proactive approach to addressing the needs of America's churches. Not only is it committed to planting and multiplying churches in America and abroad as mentioned in chapter 6, but it is also involved in assisting its established churches and those outside the denomination.

It accomplishes this through two programs. One is their national network of Disciplemaking Training Centers called T-NET. This program is designed for churches that need a challenge. Its purpose is to equip pastors and lay leaders for more effective involvement in the ministry of disciplemaking in the local church. Training tracks are offered in four areas: leadership, evangelism, education, and student ministries. The second program is church consultation. This involves sending individual consultants into struggling churches to conduct a standard evaluation and help in the areas of leadership, team building, evangelism, master planning, and facilities analysis.

The Evangelical Covenant Church. Another denomination that encourages its churches in renewal is the Evangelical

Covenant Church. It is included in chapter 6 because of its emphasis on church planting. In the 1970s, the Covenant Church created a Department of Church Growth and named Delmar Anderson as one of the first directors of church growth on a denominational level in America. They have raised several million dollars through a Giving for Growing program that has gone toward helping their churches.

The Church of the Nazarene. A third denomination that has given significant attention to church renewal as well as church planting is the Church of the Nazarene, also mentioned in chapter 6. Early in the 1980s, it created a Division of Church Growth. The director is Bill Sullivan, who introduced church growth principles to the denomination as district superintendent in North Carolina.

Other denominations. In response to decline, some other mainline churches such as the Presbyterians and Episcopalians have begun to show interest in renewal and growth. So far this has primarily taken the form of providing church growth seminars for interested churches.

Retail Institutes

A part of the influential Church Growth Movement of the 1970s was the development of retail institutes. Their purpose is to provide churches with practical resources for renewal and church growth at reasonable cost. We will look at two.

The Institute for American Church Growth. In the early seventies, Win Arn pioneered one of the first institutes to help churches in their disciplemaking task—the Institute for American Church Growth in Pasadena, California. Along with his son, Charles, he has provided the United States and Canada with helpful materials such as 16 mm color films, videos, books, curriculum, church action training kits, along with numerous seminars and personalized consultation. In particular, he has developed a program for individual churches called the "10-Month Process" that includes a churchwide seminar, consultation, special resource kits, and personalized training all geared toward a long-term growth pattern in a key ministry area of the church's life.

The Charles E. Fuller Institute of Evangelism and Church Growth. In the midseventies, John Wimber founded the Charles E. Fuller Institute to provide consultation for church growth. Later, Wimber turned the institute over to Carl George, who has developed it into a significant cutting-edge organization. George's most recent contribution is the Meta-Church concept, which is a comprehensive approach to developing a social architecture for unlimited church growth. The institute's mission is to partner with leaders in their personal development in ministry. To accomplish this, it provides numerous seminars, Meta-Church clusters, church consultation, books, subscription tape programs, video and audio tapes, curriculum, and computer software.

Independent and Dependent Agencies

Also, a number of independent and dependent agencies have sprung up that are addressing the areas of church growth and renewal. Each brings a slightly different emphasis to the topic.

The independent agencies. Some of the independent agencies are The Leadership Network of Tyler, Texas, led by Fred Smith; Church Growth Designs of Nashville, Tennessee, led by Ron Lewis; Church Growth Center of Corunna, Indiana, led by Kent Hunter; the Center for Church Growth of Houston, Texas, led by Joseph Schubert; Church Resource Ministries of Fullerton, California, led by Sam Metcalf; and Church Growth Institute of Lynchburg, Virginia, led by Elmer Towns.

Worthy of note is the Arrow Vision (Isa. 49:2) of Leighton Ford Ministries that seeks to provide training for young leaders (ages 25–40) in the areas of leadership and evangelism.

Noting that Christianity is undergoing a major worldwide leadership transition in which the outstanding Christian leaders who emerged after World War II are ready to pass the leadership baton to a new, younger generation of leaders, Leighton Ford has caught a vision for training this new generation to accept that leadership baton. Simply stated, the vision is to help young leaders to lead more *like* Jesus and to lead more *to* Jesus. In particular, Leighton Ford Ministries seeks to develop tomorrow's Christian leaders in three foundational areas: sharpening their vision, shaping their values, and sharing their venture. At the core is the *Arrow Leadership Program*, an intensive, non-residential, two-year program designed to focus on a select group of young leaders. Other programs include Evangelism Leadership Seminars, Peer Group Gatherings, Ministry Teams, and Consulting.

The dependent agencies. A number of dependent agencies have sprung up as well. They are dependent in the sense that they are related in some way to an organization such as a church or school. One is the Center for Church Renewal of Plano, Texas, led by Gene Getz. The center is related to Fellowship Bible Church North of Plano, Texas, where Getz is the pastor. Another is the Willow Creek Association. It was founded in 1992 by Willow Creek Community Church near Chicago, Illinois, to help churches with ministries targeted to seekers. It is a not-for-profit organization staffed by people from the church. A third is the Center for Christian Leadership of Dallas, Texas, under the leadership of Howard Hendricks. It is a part of the ministry of Dallas Theological Seminary.

Individual Churches

The denominations, retail institutes, independent and dependent agencies have made a significant contribution to the revitalization of America's churches. God has raised them up to help America's churches through the latter half of the twentieth century. However, in many ways they represent a top-down effort in terms of the denominations and an outside-in effort on the part of the institutes and agencies. The leadership at the top or on the outside has caught a vision for church renewal and growth. As with church planting, the critical concern is whether or not the grassroots churches will catch a vision for revitalization. Several have, and provide excellent models for other churches.

Wooddale Church of Eden Prairie, Minnesota. Wooddale Church makes this list of model churches as well as the one in chapter 6 on church planting. Before it launched its excellent program for church planting, it experienced a time of renewal and growth. Since arriving at Wooddale more than a decade ago, Leith Anderson, its pastor, has led the church through a significant revitalization process that has brought it to megachurch status—three thousand members. In fact, it was out of this experience that Anderson has penned two excellent, popular books on change: *Dying for Change* and *A Church for the 21st Century,* which detail much of his thinking and some of the principles that led to the church's growth.

Wooddale represents an ideal model for the North American church. Not that they all necessarily become megachurches, but that they catch a vision for change, accomplish that change, and begin to aggressively plant churches in the community.

Bear Valley Baptist Church of Denver, Colorado. Another excellent model of renewal and growth is Bear Valley Baptist Church. For example, in 1970 approximately one hundred people were active in the church with a total income of $16,000. By 1982, over one thousand people were active with an income of over half-a-million dollars.[42] However, other churches have grown as fast or even faster. The unique feature at Bear Valley is how it has accomplished its revitalization and growth.

Its renewal has primarily involved turning the church from an inward to an outward focus. The strategy involved getting its people out into vital ministry across the city of Denver rather than expanding its church facilities. Though its facilities are small and cramped (the sanctuary originally seated 275), they have served as a launching pad from which more than one thousand people have been unleashed to move out into the city to serve and witness through multiple ministries such as a girls' home; a refugee center; an outreach to street people, ex-convicts, prostitutes, cult members, and so on.

Irving Bible Church of Irving, Texas. A third model of renewal is Irving Bible Church in northwest suburban Dallas. Over the years, this church has been pastored by a number of excellent men such as Chuck Swindoll and Dr. Stanley Toussaint. However, under the leadership of Andrew McQuitty, the church has transitioned over the last five years from a small, traditional Bible church to a more contemporary approach, with the result that twice it has doubled in size.

However, the church is not satisfied with simply maintaining the status quo. Instead, it has adopted a proactive stance and continues to evaluate its ministry needs to become increasingly effective in the twenty-first century. Consequently, it has focused on two problems. One is providing an ever-improving quality of care for its ever-increasing pool of people. The other is a question raised by its rapid growth: Is it growing biblically by evangelization and discipleship or merely by reshuffling the sheep from other churches in the area? After a serious evaluation of its current ministry, the church leadership has decided to shift to the Meta-Church model.[43] Pastor McQuitty believes that the Meta-Church concept will provide not only a structure to handle growth but a way of thinking that will facilitate better pastoral care and outreach to those who do not know Christ.

As with church planting, this is meant to be only a small representative sampling. A number of excellent churches exist across the nation that have accomplished effective revitalization. Also, there are other agencies and some denominations that are not mentioned here.

Food for Thought

1. What are some significant changes you have witnessed in the last few years? How much has change affected your life?
2. Are conservative churches actually growing? Why or why not?
3. Draw a line down the center of a sheet of paper. Write the term *Functions* on top of the left side. Write *Forms* on the other side. List your church's functions on the left side and match each with the forms they take on the right. How long have these forms served their functions? How might they be changed in light of the culture of your community?
4. Are you convinced that churches can change? How about your church? Must it change? Why or why not?
5. Where would you like to see change take your church? What would it look like if this happened?
6. What kind of leaders are good at leading churches through change? Are you that kind of leader? If you are a layperson, is your pastor that kind of leader?
7. Which renewal characteristics are true of your church? If these do not change, what are the chances that your church will experience revitalization?
8. If you are a denominational church, does your denomination provide help in the area of church renewal? If yes, what help is available?
9. Have you used any of the materials provided by the Institute for American Church Growth or the Charles E. Fuller Institute? If so, what? If not, why not?
10. Are there any churches in your community that are known for their program of renewal? If yes, how might they be of help to you?

8

Renewing Theological Education
Confessions of a Seminary Professor

* Do you believe that seminaries are training people adequately for ministry in the 1990s and the twenty-first century? If you are a seminary graduate, do you feel adequately trained?
* Given its limitations, can a seminary prepare a Christian for vocational ministry, or is this promising or asking too much?
* Would you consider attending a seminary for ministry training? If not, where would you seek training?
* Does your church relate in any way with a theological seminary? For example, does it give financial support, train interns, send students, and so on?

*B*ill Smith had graduated from seminary with high honors. In fact, he won two awards for the best work at the seminary in apologetics and in the Bible Department. It had not been easy because he was married and held down a part-time job as a computer programer at an insurance brokerage firm. On numerous occasions his wife complained that he always had his head in the books leaving him with little time for her. When graduation came, they both felt a strong sense of relief as they anticipated a quiet but fruitful ministry in a small church not far from their hometown. However, Bill did not make the grade in his first church, and he won no awards. In fact, he flunked out. His dwindling congregation soon became disillusioned with his academic credentials and the fact that he could sight-read the Old and New Testaments in the original languages. They just wanted somebody to lead them and, most of all, to love and care about them. They could not comprehend his sermons that failed to connect with life as they knew it. Some could not understand why he rarely visited them and seemed so aloof and inaccessible. His wife overheard a lady say, "Pastor Bill would make a good professor. He likes to read and study all the time, but he doesn't like to be around people."

When the board asked him to resign, he was devastated and angry. Did they not appreciate the fact that he was trained to think theologically? Apparently they were not aware of all the time he spent in his study pouring over his commentaries and preparing precise, accurate sermons. But what would he do now? The small church his parents attended had expressed some interest, or he might apply for the doctoral program back at the school. During his seminary years, he had become fascinated with academics. And on more than one occasion, he caught himself talking and dreaming with other seminarians of pursuing a doctoral degree and someday teaching at a seminary.

The difficult question to ask in this situation is, Who really flunked—Bill Smith or the seminary that prepared him for ministry? Perhaps the answer is *both*. Regardless, Bill did not graduate from seminary prepared for ministry as the catalog had promised when he first applied. And Bill Smith's seminary is not alone. In fact, the crucial question being asked early in the decade of the 1990s is, Will theological education survive this decade?

Almost all agree that it will not survive in its present form. The issue centers not around the need for the renewal of theological education but on how much renewal. There are lots of views. One argues that seminaries as institutions cannot prepare leaders adequately for ministry in the twenty-first century and will be replaced by alternative forms such as apprenticeship programs similar to the youth apprenticeship system in Germany,[1] teaching churches that hold pastoral conferences,[2] church-based theological education like BILD, International,[3] and so on. Another view has developed nontraditional, dynamic schools such as Seminary of the East[4] and Chesapeake Seminary[5] that are training leaders in local church facilities. A third view argues that schools could do the job, but they have become so institutionalized that it is doubtful they will change, at least not without a lot of heel dragging. If they fail to change, a fourth warns that the larger American churches—the megachurches—will replace them with their own schools.

What has happened in theological education to proliferate these alternative views? Is there truly a need to revitalize seminary education, and if so, why? This chapter will attempt to answer these questions and suggest some solutions. It will focus on some (not all) of the areas that are vital to the function of a theological school such as its purpose, faculty, students, curriculum, finances, and relationship to the church.

The Seminary and Its Purpose

Just as the church must know and pursue its purpose,[6] so must the seminary. Is the seminary's purpose to prepare people for pastoral ministry? Is it to produce professors for Bible colleges and seminaries? Is it to attract a sufficient number of students to pay the bills? Is it to educate laypeople? Is it to train world Christians?

The purpose of theological seminaries has varied somewhat depending on such factors as the school's theological stance (liberal or conservative), the school's financial condition, its emphasis on academics, and so on. Some view the seminary's purpose as primarily vocational and gender exclusive—to prepare men for pastoral ministry in America's churches. Indeed, the growing demand for pastoral preparation in the past has produced the bread-and-butter programs that have paid the bills in most institutions. Many churches were planted and grew in the first half of the century—especially in the 1950s when America was largely a churched culture. The seminaries sought to provide the professional training and intellectual preparation for men of faith who either were already in ministry or felt God was calling them to pastor these churches.

Others view the purpose of the seminary as broad and intellectual. Richard Niebuhr has stated that the ultimate purpose of the theological college in the West was to be "the intellectual centre of the church's life."[7] This is still the purpose of many of the faculty who view the theological institution as a place to pursue the kind of scholarship that is vital to Christianity but is not possible in the typical church.

However, Paul Stevens responds to Niebuhr's purpose for the theological college with the observation that "Niebuhr's stated purpose is being questioned from inside and outside academia: outside by the church which is not sure it needs and wants an intellectual centre, and inside by the theological college which is no longer sure that its primary purpose is to help the church think biblically and critically."[8]

While it is true that a theological seminary is a place to pursue scholarly biblical and theological studies, Stevens observes, "It is not surprising that students find themselves enthralled with scholarship and lose interest in pastoral or evangelistic ministry, or involvement in society."[9] A quick perusal of most seminary catalogs reveals a curriculum where the academic clearly holds sway over the practical, and there are few if any courses on evangelism. In addition, Stevens accurately laments the truth that many students "experience graduate theological education as a spiritual wasteland during the time they submit to the rigors of academia, exams, research assignments and academic hierarchies."[10]

Along this same line, some seminaries have had to make a decision as to whether they want to function as graduate schools of religion, focusing solely on academics, or as professional schools, preparing men and women for Christian ministry. It appears that many have opted for the latter. Leith Anderson comments, "Few schools have the resources to train both. We will need comparatively few graduate schools of theology and comparatively more professional schools of ministry. Both must move away from the traditional notion of education being time and space, but this switch must especially apply to the preparation of practitioners. They want to be (and the church wants) men and women who can do something, not know everything."[11]

The larger seminaries in the 1990s do not see their primary purpose as training pastors exclusively for the local church. The fact is that as the century draws to a close, fewer people are going into pastoral ministry. Also, the majority of pastors who are seminary graduates serve America's small churches, while more than one-third of the senior pastors leading the megachurches do not have a seminary degree.[12] This has prompted Lyle Schaller to ask, "Will the future role of the theological seminaries be to educate students to serve the shrinking number of small churches that can barely afford a full-time pastor?"[13]

The movement in urban America is away from the small churches to the more attractive ministry menus of the larger, full-service churches. If this continues, there will be no small churches for seminary graduates to pastor. Consequently, seminaries have opened their doors to both men and women interested in a general knowledge of the Bible and theology and other areas of vocational ministry such as counseling. Few seminaries, however, have caught a vision for providing theological education for the layperson.

The time-worn cliché of biting off more than you can chew describes the problem facing the purpose of the theological seminary. Seminaries are promising too much—much more than they can possibly deliver. Stevens puts the problem in its proper context by distinguishing between the goal of theological education and the purpose of the theological institution:

> Undoubtedly part of the confusion is caused by a failure to distinguish between the goal of theological education and the purpose of the theological college. Theological education is the lifelong process of forming Christian persons into the maturity of Christ and equipping them to serve God's purposes in the church and world. A theological college can only engage a part of that purpose, a truth usually not appreciated by incoming students. In the West the confusion is problematic; overseas it is debilitating confusion as newer churches without an evolved history of theological education try to make their Bible schools and theological colleges perform the *whole* task of theological education.[14]

Seminaries make a major mistake when they promise to prepare people for ministry. This confuses the goal of theological education with the purpose of the theological school. The result is that the seminary cannot possibly deliver on its promise. When students graduate and pursue various ministries, they discover this truth and feel cheated. An example is the pastorate. Many seminaries have done a good job of providing future pastors with a knowledge of the Bible, the original languages, church history, and so on. However, they have provided little if any training in the spiritual life, leadership, culture, evangelism, and other practical essentials for ministry.

Consequently, they should not speak of preparing leaders for ministry. Instead, they must talk in terms of equipping leaders to begin the lifelong process of theological education.

If the seminary decides to continue to emphasize the more academic areas to the exclusion of the practical essentials, it is imperative that it communicate this clearly to incoming students so that they do not graduate naively thinking that they are prepared for ministry in today's secular culture.

In addition, theological schools will need to aggressively pursue programs that will promote and provide lifelong learning for their graduates. These opportunities should not only keep them abreast of changes and recent developments in academics but should enable them to evaluate and retool while involved in ministry. To a limited degree, this is currently taking place in some institutions through the doctor of ministry programs and continuing education. However, many graduates are looking for much more than is currently being envisioned.

The Seminary and Its Faculty

Perhaps the most important ingredient of any educational institution, whether secular or theological, graduate or undergraduate, private or public, is the faculty. As the faculty goes, so goes the institution. No theological school will ever rise above the gifts and abilities of its faculty. All else—the administration, curriculum, facilities—either helps or hinders a good teacher but could never supplant him or her. In short, the teachers of an institution set the pace for that institution.[15]

The faculties of America's seminaries have drawn more criticism than praise in the late 1980s and early 1990s, especially from the nation's churches who question how well they have prepared their students for ministry in today's world. Their complaints are multiple. First, faculties are widely perceived as too theoretical and thus out of touch with reality. Some view them as unable to address the real issues of people in the 1990s who are facing the third millennium.

Much of this is attributed to the fact that they spend so much of their time in the Christian womb—behind a closed door in an isolated, academic environment located on a Christian campus.

Seminary faculties are seen as working off old academic models of the classical European universities of yesterday's world that no longer adequately prepare students of today's world for significant ministry in tomorrow's world. For example, they are producing pastors like Bill Smith who can conjugate nouns, parse verbs, and recite from memory all the Hebrew irregular verbs. However, graduates have no preparation in the ministry essentials such as leadership, the spiritual life, and so on. This is attributed to the fact that many faculties appear generally unaware of all the cultural changes in today's society and the ministries of significant, innovative churches sprinkled across America. Instead, when faced with change and innovation, they seem to be retrenching and protecting worn departmental turf at all costs.

There is also concern over their people skills. Some view them as scholars who prefer the quiet, academic life hidden away in some office doing research. Most often the response is that this kind of work is vital to Christianity and the promotion and preservation of the faith—which is true. Others point out, however, that these men are role models for the pastors of the nation's future churches (at least the small churches) where people skills are essential—as Bill Smith may or may not have learned.

Another major concern is the faculty's lack of practical experience, especially in churches. Critics argue that a faculty that is preparing men and women for ministry in the church needs to have much current, practical experience in the church. When this is the case, the classroom takes on a ministry flavor that integrates subject matter with real life in the ministry world.

A survey of most theological faculties will reveal that the majority have little if any practical, outside-the-seminary experience. Few have ever pastored a church. Teaching Sunday school classes or preaching in churches on the weekends is helpful but does not provide the experience necessary to gain a feel for what is taking place in America's congregations. Consequently, much of what a teacher does in the classroom is too theoretical and divorced from the reality of congregational life. Obviously, the same would apply to parachurch ministries as well.

Several changes have been suggested or predicted for seminary faculties in the future. One would provide faculties with excellent opportunities for needed practical experience. It suggests a new approach as to how and where they spend their sabbaticals. Presently, most use this time away from their immmediate faculty responsibilities either to write or travel. Paul Stevens suggests, "Faculty could prepare to be better educators by considering some life-changing and challenging alternatives for a sabbatical: becoming a theologian-in-residence in a business, doing research in a Third World college, living among the poor, volunteering to be a part of a pastoral team in a local church or working as a theologian-in-residence in a mission context."[16]

This would help teachers remain in touch with the contexts in which their students will be ministering. It would also serve as an example of the kind of integration of theory and practice necessary to make a difference in training those who will minister in and to this pagan world.

Another change that would supply needed practical input is the use of more adjunct faculty. Not only might the faculty leave the ivory tower for ministry experience in the world, but those ministering in the world can invade the ivory tower. In an interview in *Christianity Today*, David Hubbard, the president of Fuller Theological Seminary, predicts: "In the future, we may see a third to half of education done by people engaged in some form of specialized ministry. We will probably use smaller core faculties and larger adjunct faculties. And we will be farming out more of our education to churches and other Christian agencies. They can be our laboratories."[17] Contrary to past practice, these adjunct faculty members need to be involved much more in faculty and departmental meetings with voting privileges and to have much input into the future direction of the institution.

Some suggest that a third change should be the elimination of faculty tenure. They believe that the practice of granting professors long-term contracts should be dropped. Instead, they argue that faculty members should sign short-term contracts based on performance and the accomplishment of stated teaching, ministry, or research goals. It is true that tenure has served to protect faculty from capricious, indiscriminate administrators. But it has also served to protect teachers who are entrenched in old paradigms or who fight turf battles contrary to the vision and mission of the theological institution.

The Seminary and Its Students

As important as the faculty is to quality theological education, they would not be necessary if the school had no students. In fact, some schools have experienced a decline in the number of students, which has resulted in the release of a number of their faculty.

A decided shift has taken place in the kinds of students pursuing theological education in the 1990s. In the past, many were single and came straight from the secular or Bible college campus to seminary. They were young, biblically articulate, and predominantly white males who lived on campus. Many considered them our best and brightest, with a burning passion to serve the Savior in some type of vocational Christian ministry, most likely the pastorate. They came from predominantly Christian families and were willing to take the time to pursue a three-year program such as the master of divinity or a four-year program such as the master of theology.

Today these kinds of students are a minority. The profile of the average student has changed in many ways. The first affects age, gender, and ethnicity. The average entering age of students, many of whom are second- and third-career people, is in the low to mid thirties. The number of women, minority students, and international students has increased. This means that students will have different demands and different expectations for their educations. Seminaries will have to make some hard choices here. Either they will need to specialize and focus on a few areas or broaden their menu to include a greater variety of programs to meet the training demands of these new students. Since the former would require massive change and the loss of many jobs on campus, the latter appears to be the preferred choice.

The profile is also changing as many feel that Christianity's best and brightest are not pursuing ministry positions in what they perceive to be old paradigm ministries. Instead, they are looking to the marketplace and elsewhere for new, exciting challenges where they can witness more effectively for Christ. Some are still opting for creative, innovative parachurch ministries. The seminaries would be wise to identify and pursue these potential leaders. They should also be cognizant of new cutting-edge ministries and encourage and train their students to think in terms of new ministry paradigms.

Another change is that many students are coming to seminary desiring shorter programs and training for positions other than the pastorate. More are pursuing a one- or two-year master of arts degree than are pursuing the master of divinity degree, and few schools offer the master of theology degree. In the early 1990s, Denver Seminary has more students pursuing its counseling program than the ministerial program. Seminaries must be more realistic as to what it takes to equip people for a given ministry. The fact that some outstanding Christian leaders never attended seminary speaks volumes. Schools must ask, What precisely is necessary to launch people into this particular ministry niche? or

What are the bare essentials? Some are guilty of confusing the goal of theological education with the purpose of a theological seminary and pack a course of study with additional, unnecessary classes that stretch three-year programs into four years and four-year programs into five and six years.

They would also be wise to ask, What new ministry niches are worthy of seminary preparation? and Do we have the necessary faculty on board to facilitate them? Outside counsel is critical in making these kinds of decisions, because schools are not always aware of what is taking place in pastoral and other ministries off campus.

The profile of a strong Christian background has changed as many come from dysfunctional and/or abusive backgrounds, not to mention difficult single-family contexts. Thus, they arrive on campus with lots of emotional baggage and limitations. This will have a deep impact on future Christian ministries. For example, dysfunctional pastors will attempt to minister to dysfunctional congregations, resulting in ministry disaster. Consequently, seminaries will need to implement spiritual formation groups, encourage faculty to be more available to students, and provide professional counselors on staff to work with these future ministry leaders.

More of today's students enter seminary with less Bible knowledge and in search of their faith. Paul Stevens writes, "But a shift has taken place in North America whereby students are now more often coming to a theological seminary not to prepare for a career in ministry but to find their own faith."[18] A variation of this problem is students using seminary to determine if they should go into vocational Christian ministry. They spend two or three years in school asking if vocational ministry is a safe career to pursue. Both these problems lead naturally to a greater number of ministry dropouts after graduation.

Seminaries would be wise to require that all new and incoming students go through an assessment process that would help them to discover their divine designs—spiritual and natural gifts, temperament, passion, and so on. This would help them to determine their ministry place in the kingdom and pursue the program that best equips them to begin the process. If a faith struggle is taking place, the assessor would quickly pick up on it, identify it for the student, and prescribe a course of action to help the student work through his or her faith journey.

The Seminary and Its Curriculum

An important question that those involved in the educational process must ask is: Can the theological seminary adequately train a person for future ministry? An important part of the answer looks to the curriculum.

Much criticism of late has been directed at the course of study at the typical theological seminary. Leith Anderson calls attention to some of the inadequacies in preparing people for ministry in the church. He writes:

There is a growing realization that classical theological education has not appropriately prepared men and women for leadership in late twentieth-century American churches. . . . Much theological education is based on the "academy model" of classical European universities. Students are trained to be scholars. They are given the tools for research and analysis, and then are trained to be theoretical theologians. Certainly there is a need for such specialized training. Without careful scholarship the Christian church would probably repeat the heresies of earlier eras within a generation.

The rub comes when graduates face the realities of parish ministry. There is little time for the more leisurely life of scholarship. People aren't asking for academic alternatives, they are expecting practical answers to life's problems. Too often the pastor is like an emergency-room physician trained in genetic research but surrounded by patients with gunshot wounds.[19]

One explanation for this is that some seminaries encourage their academic faculty to pursue advanced degrees in classical European institutions that perpetuate the academy model. This can be an overwhelming academic experience in what is an unreal world that permanently marks teachers' lives and is passed on to their students. Unfortunately, this kind of training, though valuable, does not seem to have appreciably advanced the cause of Christianity in the European countries in which it originated and is still being offered. In fact, Europe is considered a spiritual wasteland in terms of Christianity.[20]

While seminaries have excelled with curricula for training scholars who function well in isolation, ministry in the local church calls for abilities and creative skills in leadership as well as scholarship. These skills affect how leaders impact people. Lyle Schaller observes:

> By definition, leadership exists in a social setting that includes other people. Leaders do not exist in complete isolation from other people. One of the frequent complaints by the laity about their pastor is, "Our minister probably should have been a professor rather than a pastor. He likes to read and study and to work on sermons, but he really doesn't like to be around people. . . ." Scholarship and leadership are not incompatible attributes—look at Theodore Roosevelt—but they are different traits. Scholarship can exist in isolation from people, but leadership happens only in the context of a social setting with people."[21]

Also, Jay Conger quotes Robert Altmeyer's Carnegie-Mellon doctoral dissertation on the different styles of thinking. He gives evidence that indicates that a curriculum strong in analytic skills (such as that which is prevalent in a seminary curriculum) may cause the unlearning of the imaginative skills needed for leadership.[22]

Another inadequacy is that the faculties set the direction and establish the curricula of most theological institutions.

The problem is their pastoral model. Bruce Shelley observes: "The image of the pastor-theologian is the ideal for most theological faculties. . . ."[23] The pastor-theologian is one who functions as a scholar within the four walls of the church. As theologian, he spends most of his day in the study using the original languages to exegete the Scriptures in preparation for teaching God's people on Sunday morning. Because he knows how to think theologically, chances are good that his church will not drift into false teaching.[24] His studies are interrupted only by such pastoral responsibilities as hospital visits and an occasional wedding or funeral. Shelley says this model is "no longer widely popular."[25] I would add that it is no longer widely practical or possible in today's church struggling for lack of strong leadership in a secular climate.

The current demands on pastors focus on such areas as leadership, communication, people skills, exegeting the culture, and the training of lay leaders in addition to the ability to exegete Scripture and to think theologically. The former is just as biblical as the latter—Scripture has much to say about the importance of spiritual leadership, godly people skills, and so on. It is not an either-or relationship, it is a both-and relationship. Add to all this the truth that the concept of ministry has vastly changed over the last three decades, and it becomes imperative that schools address these needs in the curriculum. Seminaries have gained a reputation for preparing people to minister in a world that no longer exists—the world of the 1950s, not the twenty-first century.

The question is, Can these more practical elements of the curriculum be learned in the seminary setting? Many would answer, No. They see the future of theological education moving toward a partnership between the seminaries and local churches. Practically every article I have read recently concerning the future of seminary education alludes to the need for seminaries and churches to partner together in the preparation of men and women for ministry. For example, Leith

Anderson writes, "New formats are now developing in which churches and schools work together in training clergy; schools emphasize theory while churches emphasize practice. Internships and 'field education' are being added to the curriculum. The student then implements theory in a practical setting of a church under the guidance and supervision of one with experience."[26]

Though practical ministry involvement and field education have been part of the curriculum of most seminaries, it has played an insignificant role in a context where scholarship reigns. The new format is to devote more of the curriculum to the practical essentials and do much of it in a local church environment. The emphasis is on a field-based, church-based informal setting as opposed to what at present is essentially a classroom-based formal setting. In *The Leadership Challenge*, Professors Kouzes and Posner point to the inadequacies of attempting to train leaders in a formal educational setting alone. They rate it a distant third in terms of learning effectiveness.[27]

This does not mean, however, that the seminaries should hand off all the practical essentials to the church and focus on theory alone. The seminary must model more than the intellectual dimension of ministry. Stevens writes: "Indeed, the college has a responsibility for modeling the integration of mind, heart, spirit and action that ought to obtain in a lifelong experience of learning and growing in Christian discipleship and service."[28] Instead, the seminary must work along with the church. A number of churches are dysfunctional and would cause more harm than good; some pastors are excellent leaders and communicators of biblical truth but do not know how to mentor students. The need for quality control will always be present.

A final inadequacy is what I refer to as the pedagogical "cognitive dump." Learning has become synonymous with taking in information. Some curricula and faculty focus on "dumping" knowledge on students to the exclusion of teaching students to think for themselves. A faculty person may have done a lot of research on a topic and delights in conveying that knowledge to his or her students. However, students need to know how professors process their information and arrive at their conclusions. It is critical that schools teach students how to fish as well as giving them fish. Both are necessary, but the former takes priority over the latter because much content will be outdated or updated in a few years.

In addition, it is not enough that faculty be theologians, they must also be educators. Many are victims of their own pedagogy[29]—they pursue academic doctoral degrees in preparation for teaching but take no courses in higher education and teaching methodology. Consequently, some have bought into a defunct linear approach to learning—first, you learn the theory, and then you graduate and put it into practice. Stevens correctly observes: "What is really needed is a spiral of learning: theory followed by *praxis* followed by reflection on theory and so on. For the seminary this boils down to the question of whether theological education must be education *for* ministry or education *in* ministry. In place of the classes and field education we need an integrated cycle of *praxis*, instruction and reflection."[30]

The Seminary and Its Finances

Like it or not, schools need money to provide a quality educational program—just ask the president of any school or his board. Unfortunately, it takes money to build or repair facilities, to hire competent staff and faculties, and to maintain equipment. Seminaries are not exempt from difficult financial times characterized by escalating costs. Though denominationally related schools are not exempt from financial problems, this section focuses more on schools that are not funded by a particular denominational body.

The primary financial sources for most independent seminaries are student tuition and donor giving. According to the Association of Theological Schools, the average full-time student in a graduate theological institution in America pays approximately $16,000 per year.[31] David Hubbard speaks for many seminaries when he says of Fuller Seminary's tuition costs, "We are at a level where students just cannot earn enough money to pay for it. I believe we're close to peaking on tuition raises."[32]

In order to cope with rising tuition costs, many students spread their schooling out over a longer period of time, taking fewer hours per semester. The result is they are in school longer, delaying their entrance into the ministry for which they are preparing. Also, the added time and expense places more strain on the average married student's family life. The spouse has to work longer, and the student's spouse and children will have less time with him or her because of seminary obligations. All of this coupled with the low entry-level income of most church or parachurch ministries makes it exceedingly difficult for students to afford a quality seminary education.

The problem is that many seminaries are becoming more dependent on student tuition than donor giving. The donor base appears to be shrinking. The Pre-Boomers are aging, many are retiring on fixed incomes or have died. Churches also are experiencing financial difficulties as they face a decline in members. Many have had to drop their support of missions and schools to cover their own financial shortfalls. Others have lost confidence in the seminaries and their ability to train men and women for effective ministry in today's secular climate. The effectiveness of direct mail is on a plateau or in decline, and more schools are becoming increasingly competitive, forcing seminaries to share more of the economic pie.

The extent to which a seminary can continue to operate in the present economic situation is highly suspect. If student tuition climbs any higher, theological education will become unavailable for the majority of students in North America and practically impossible for some minorities and international students. Today's Baby Boomers and Busters give their finances in different ways and for different reasons. The new givers are not as committed as past contributors to faithfully supporting institutions, especially those operating in the red. They are predisposed to give to ministries that cast strong visions to meet needs rather than giving to the needs themselves.

David Hubbard believes that a big part of the answer lies in endowments. "Seminaries need affluent people to step up and lay large gifts on the table to subsidize student aid and to subsidize programs. Some schools with a denominational backing have been able to go to their denominations for a little more support. But we really need permanent support. And that's where endowments are critical."[33]

Hubbard is correct, but seminaries in these difficult times need strong, innovative leadership at the top that is capable of casting and implementing a significant, powerful vision for the future. Baby Boomers tend to be cynics, and Baby Busters are apathetic. Leadership will need to acknowledge the problems with *what is* in theological education and begin to talk in terms of *what could be* if they are to survive the present and future economic dilemma.

There are some leaders in schools across America who have turned failing institutions around. An example is Dr. Gary Cook at Dallas Baptist University, located in southwest Dallas, Texas. When he took office, he inherited a fiscally impossible situation—a school with a $6 million deficit, buildings in disrepair, and dorms with empty rooms. Though not without much controversy, during his five-year tenure he has led the school to a position where all its bills are paid, its enrollment is at a new high, it has begun a $1 million renovation of classrooms, and it showcases a new $4.5 million debt-free student center.[34] Theological institutions need to study these renewed schools and ask questions such as, What did they do? and What kind of leaders does it take to renew declining institutions? I believe that strong leadership will play a major role in winning back America's churches and attracting the new donors for the cause of theological education.

The Seminary and the Church

At the turn of the century, only a handful of churches existed in North America that ministered to a thousand people or more at worship. Today, all that has changed. There are thousands of megachurches with a thousand or more worshippers, and the end is not yet in sight. The emergence of the megachurch is one of the more significant developments on the contemporary American church scene.

According to Lyle Schaller, the megachurch phenomenon poses several problems for seminaries. The first, as stated earlier, is that more than one third of the megachurch pastors do not have seminary degrees.[35] Does this foreshadow a trend away from seminary preparation for ministry? If so, where will future large-church pastors learn the orthodox faith? The second is that megachurches increasingly are turning to promising, gifted laypeople in their congregations to fill staff positions rather than seminary graduates. They complain that it takes too long for seminarians to get over seminary and become ministry-effective. This could mean that megachurches, not seminaries, will provide the staff for tomorrow's larger churches. Finally, the increasing number of megachurches and the diminishing number of small churches means fewer jobs for seminary graduates at a time when placement offices are bulging with resumes but have few places to send them.[36]

Another problem is the suspicion of both megachurch pastors and seminary professors toward one another. On the one hand, the pastors seem to place a premium on character and performance rather than credentials and see much of seminary training as too scholarly and irrelevant to the church. Their primary concern is pragmatic, Can a person get the job done? On the other hand, the professors place a priority on knowing. Their primary concern is intellectual, What do you know? Can you articulate the orthodox faith of the Scriptures?

In the past, the seminaries held sway over the churches. Most churches were small and looked to the larger schools for recognition and encouragement. In the process, they sensed feelings of independence and arrogance from some schools. In effect, the churches revolved around the seminaries. Today, with the megachurch phenomenon, the shoe has changed feet. Many churches are bigger than the seminaries and project a we-don't-need-you attitude, while some pastors show arrogance toward theological institutions.

The solution seems fairly obvious and has been touched on earlier. Whether they realize it or not, the seminaries need the churches and the churches need the seminaries. The real need is for the seminaries to partner with churches in providing practical, relevant, theological education that is true to the Scriptures and preserves the orthodox faith. Both have much to offer the other, and both (especially the seminaries) will need to make some changes before this will happen.

Stevens argues that the seminaries need to go to the churches. "A balance of residential community and extension programs seems not only to be the inevitable shape of the future but the best of all possible educational worlds."[37] There are several advantages. First, students do not have to leave their ministries to pursue a theological education. Second, students can learn in ministry by applying their studies to their ministries. Third, it is easier to send a faculty person to an extension center than to require several hundred students to pick up, leave their lives behind, and move to a new residential community. Fourth, by staying in ministry, a congregation or parachurch ministry may be able to help defray some of the financial costs.

Most agree that these are not good times for theological schools that cling to past paradigms. An example used throughout this chapter is the school's preparation of people for pastoral ministry in the nation's churches. The typical seminary has for years equipped pastors with the skills necessary to lead small churches in a more rural, Christian-friendly environment. Over the past few decades, all of this has changed significantly, and there is a desperate need to equip pastors with a new set of skills to lead larger churches in what has become a largely unchurched, urban world. Much the same is true for parachurch ministry. The question remains, Will the seminaries rise to the occasion and make the changes necessary to accomplish this feat?

Essentially, they have two choices. One is not to change. This choice views the future much as a continuation of the past. It argues, "If it ain't broke, don't fix it!" It asks the question, What is all the fuss about? Things aren't so bad; after all, we've managed to survive this far with only a few small changes along the way. It confides, What we really need to do is return to the way we did things around here in the good old days. This is the same choice that the ostrich makes when it buries its head in the sand and thinks all is well when in fact it has never been more vulnerable.

The other choice is to realize that the past is history and the future will be radically different. It argues, "If you think it ain't broke, then you must be living on another planet." It asks the questions, What is holding us back? How have we managed to survive all these years with so few changes along the way? It confides, What we really need to do is not to return to the good old days but to return to what made the good old days good—biblical fidelity, strong leadership, vision, innovation, and creativity. This is the same choice that the lead goose makes in a flock of Canada geese when they migrate north for the winter. As a servant, it picks the straightest, best route and leads the way, at great risk to itself, recognizing its dependence on the others in the flock if they are ever to accomplish their mission as a team.

The first choice is passive. If seminaries decide not to change or to change at a snail's pace, then the decision regarding their future will be made for them. The second choice is proactive. It allows the school to decide if it has a future and to determine and shape that future.

Food for Thought

1. Do you know someone like Pastor Bill Smith, a recent seminary graduate who did not last very long in his first ministry? If yes, what were the circumstances?
2. Have you attended or graduated from a theological seminary? If yes, did you find that you were prepared for ministry? Why or why not? Were your expectations and/or the school's reasonable?
3. What is your initial perception of a seminary or Christian college faculty? Do you know any faculty persons in a school environment? If yes, has your initial perception of them changed as you have gotten to know them better? How have they not changed?
4. Do you know any students of a seminary or Christian college? How are they like the changing students described in this chapter? How are they different?
5. Does your church support a seminary or Christian college? Why or why not? Do you support a seminary or college? Why or why not?
6. What is your church's attitude toward the theological seminary in general? What is your pastor's attitude? Are the two different or the same? Does either believe that seminaries are out of touch with America's churches? Why or why not?

Epilogue
A Look into the Future

To say that life has changed drastically for Bobby, LaTonya, and Brian over the last ten years is to be guilty of understatement. In a decade of mega-change, since we were first introduced to them, the years have brought tumultuous change, most of which has been good to them. Bobby still works out regularly and remains tall and trim, but at age forty-six, he is showing a swath of distinguished gray around the ears. Having finished his medical degree in 1997, he has found his niche in life and is practicing medicine as a vascular surgeon in Dallas, Texas.

Bobby's income is such that he no longer has to keep bar part-time as he did when immersed in his studies as a medical student. But he readily admits that he misses it. He simply enjoys being around and helping people. As a bartender, you do a lot of listening, and after a year, he began to realize that in spite of all their specialized training and prominence in the health-care profession, doctors and nurses hurt like anyone else. Life is no respecter of persons, and tragedy falls on the famous and the infamous alike.

Judith is gone. The last he heard, she was living with another attorney who works with her in the D.A.'s office. Bobby and Judith lived together for three years, which was long enough for them to realize that they were not compatible. At first, life for them went unusually well. They both made enough money to live the good life. But as they settled into that life together, various childhood emotional splinters began to work their way to the surface. All the Dallas Mavericks' basketball games, the neighborhood projects, and tutoring the inner-city kids were not enough to save the relationship. It eventually blew apart, and they went their separate ways, hurt but amicable.

The "big event," as Bobby affectionately labeled it, was a part of the reason for the death of their relationship. While working out during medical school, Bobby met Bill, who was about his age and was planting a church for "people who don't like church" in a Dallas suburb. When he discovered that Bill was in the ministry, he attempted to keep him at a distance. But Bill had a way of "getting into your life," as Bobby expressed it, and in time they began to work out together. Though Bill was different, Bobby liked him, and it was only a matter of time before he gave in and attended a small, informal seeker's Bible study that Bill taught for a group of doctors and their wives who desired to reach out to those in their profession.

Though he had anticipated the worst, he was impressed with these people and the critical issues they discussed. He had no idea that the Bible was relevant to life in the 1990s. What he had assumed would be a boring one-time event, turned into a year of numerous questions and much soul-searching as he began to seek God. The "big event" took place one year to the day after he first attended the study. He became convinced deep in his soul that Christ was the answer to his life, and late one night after he and Bill talked into the early hours of the morning, he embraced Christ as his Savior.

Judith began to attend some of the studies with Bobby. However, she admitted that she was never comfortable around "those people" and a bit skeptical of the Bible study itself. In time, she stopped attending altogether. And when Bobby accepted Christ, it was the last straw. Bobby suspected that in light of their personal problems, she was already seeing another man and was not seriously considering the claims of authentic Christianity. Regardless, when Bobby told her of his decision for Christ, she packed her bags, and the relationship was history.

At present, Bobby is working as a layman with Bill in the planting of the new paradigm church—the kind of church that will attract people just like Bobby. The ministry is not yet a year old, and already 125 people are attending the morning services, many of whom have recently accepted Christ. Bobby has taken over the study with the medical community, and a significant number of those attending the new church have come as the result of Bobby's teaching and evangelistic style. In fact, some first-time attenders have wondered if this was a church for those in the health-care profession. When he has time for reflection, Bobby thanks God for Bill and people like him who have such a passion to reach out to unchurched people. In fact, though a physician, Bobby has committed his life to the same purpose.

LaTonya no longer lives on welfare with her grandmother in the inner city of Washington, D.C. Change has had a significant impact on her life as well. Her grandmother has died, and her brothers and sisters are living on their own. Her father has disappeared, and she has not heard from him in years. She suspects that either he has been killed in a drug bust, or he is doing time in the county jail. Presently, she and her husband live together with her eleven-year-old daughter in a small black community not far from the inner-city area where she grew up.

Most of the change that has taken place in LaTonya's life began when she accepted Christ as Savior. The elderly pastor of an older, struggling African-American church near the projects retired, and a new, younger pastor was called in his place. Within a year, the new man had made a number of significant changes that served to breathe new life into this old, dying congregation. First, he sought to balance the pursuit of social justice and equality with good preaching from the Bible. The people began to understand the Scriptures in a new way, and Christ became more the focal point of the church's life. Second, although this congregation consisted predominantly of middle-class professional people who drove in to church from the suburbs where most lived, they had a desire to reach inner-city America for the Savior. And they had decided to start in their own backyard with the project where LaTonya and her grandma lived.

A group of men in the church targeted LaTonya's project and started a number of strategic Bible studies in people's apartments. In addition, one of the men who was on the city council put some pressure on the police captain responsible for drug enforcement in the projects. Dramatically, life began to change for the better. People in the project began to take heart. It seemed as if they suddenly came alive, and their hopes were rekindled. A surprising number of them began to take part in the weekend march against drugs and in the Bible studies. LaTonya was one of these. In fact, her grandmother requested that the first Bible study begin in her flat.

The church sent out a young, single man who had grown up in this very same project. Through the persistent efforts of a Christian who worked closely with the city's antigang unit, he had been confronted with authentic Christianity. In time, he came to faith and became a vital part of the revitalized church due to the active recruitment of the new pastor. One of the first people he led to Christ was LaTonya. Shortly thereafter, a wonderful, older lady in the church saw the transformation that had taken place in her soul and began to disciple her. LaTonya was so excited that she invited others to the Bible study. For the first time in her twenty-five years, she discovered that there was a purpose for her life that gave her a sense of direction and a feeling of significance.

Two years later the young man and LaTonya have married, and he has adopted her daughter. He works full time with the antigang unit and part-time for the church. LaTonya is expecting their first child and has returned to finish school. She even talks of pursuing a degree at the local community college. Most important, however, is her active involvement in discipling some of the many young women in the project who have come to faith. LaTonya has dedicated her life to reaching out to these desperate women who mirror her own past life. She is convinced that the church of Jesus Christ can make the difference in their lives and the lives of so many just like them in the inner cities of America.

Brian, now thirty-three, still finds some time in his busy schedule for basketball and plays an occasional game of pickup at the local Y. The rest of his time is spent attending a theological seminary where he is busily preparing for the ministry. As in the lives of Bobby and LaTonya, a lot has transpired over the last decade.

His mom is now the special assistant to the president of a television station that was the chief competitor of her former employer where she worked for six years as the vice president of news programming. The communications business is very competitive, and in their climb up the corporate ladder, few profess loyalty to any station or network. She has also remarried and lives with her lawyer husband and his two active teenage daughters in an affluent community on the north side of the city.

Desperate for friends, Brian eventually fell in with the wrong crowd and pursued the drug scene for several years. That is when his life began to change for the better. On occasion, he opted to sell drugs for extra money. One day the police suddenly and brutally entered the picture, and Brian narrowly missed being shot by a narc who was on his first bust. The police locked Brian up on charges of possessing and dealing in drugs. Remarkably, his stepfather was able to get the charges reduced to possession only. Brian pleaded guilty and spent six months in a community service program working intensively with five retarded kids. The near-fatal drug bust and the time with those loving, innocent kids sobered Brian considerably. He began to lie awake at night thinking about the lack of direction in his life.

Then his dad suddenly reentered the picture after a five-year absence. One day there was a knock at the door, he opened it, and there stood his dad with a big smile across his face. Instantly, Brian sensed that something was different. His dad spoke of his addiction to alcohol and how it had infected and ravaged his life and family—a story Brian knew firsthand. Most important, he spoke of his new faith in Christ and the unconditional love and care of the men in his twelve-step group at church. Brian was understandably skeptical at first, but his father continued to pursue and relate to him as never before. This son was deeply touched by his prodigal father's love.

Over a period of months, Brian began to visit his dad's church and met some men and women his age. Their faith proved authentic, and their witness coupled with his dad's unswerving testimony resulted in his coming to faith. It was dramatic—all the missing pieces to his life's puzzle seemed to fall into place. In particular, he experienced an unsatiable thirst for the Scriptures. He began to carry his small pocket Bible and read it whenever he had the opportunity. The more he studied, the greater was his thirst.

In time, Brian found himself not only actively involved in the singles' program at church, but its leader. Brian's interest was at a spiritual peak, and he began to question if perhaps some form of the ministry might be in his future. Then, the singles' pastor, who next to his dad had become his closest friend, approached him about an opening on the staff. Although he realized he might not be ready for the position, the invitation served to catalyze his decision for a lifetime of vocational ministry.

His personal study of the Scriptures, his commitment to ministry, and his leadership of the singles' group all combined to focus his desire for further studies. Consequently, Brian enrolled the following year at an excellent evangelical seminary located in the city. Not only did the pastoral staff highly recommend it, but the school had an outstanding reputation for turning out men and women who knew the Bible well and who led with sustained excellence in a variety of ministries around the world.

It was not a traditional seminary based on the classical model of the European university, however. Students were trained to be servants, not scholars or research theologians. The seminary provided studies in languages and church history, and the academic studies were tied directly to ministry. At the same time, it partnered in the students' preparation with church and parachurch ministries so that much of the students' time was spent with adjunct faculty up to their elbows in actual ministry. Students graduated with an appreciation not only for academics but for practical areas such as evangelism, leadership, and other vital ministry essentials.

Brian was not sure of all that God had in store for him during his short stay on planet earth. He was convinced, however, that based on God's amazing work thus far in his life coupled with his unique seminary preparation, he would be well prepared to offer a cold cup of water to his spiritually dry generation in the twenty-first century.

Notes

Introduction

1. I am not arguing that the country needs to return to its "biblical base" established by founding fathers who wanted a Christian America. This view is not historically accurate. Due to the First Amendment, Christian influences were strong in the birthing of the nation. However, the founding fathers, many of whom were deists, chose specifically *not* to prefer any particular religion as the basis for the new republic. Instead, they opted for a pluralist nation where anyone could pursue and practice any religion or nonreligion. *See* Mark A. Noll, Nathan Hatch, and George Marsden, *The Search for Christian America* (Westchester, Ill.: Crossway, 1983), 127–44.

Chapter 1: *The State of American Society*

1. Karen Lincoln Michel, "I Wanted to Do Something," *Dallas Morning News*, 22 February 1993.

2. Steve McGonigle, "Supreme Court Broadens Church Access to Schools," *Dallas Morning News*, 8 June 1993.

3. Mark A. Noll, *A History of Christianity in the United States*

and Canada (Grand Rapids: Eerdmans, 1992), 550.

4. Ibid., 552.

5. Noll, Hatch, and Marsden, *Christian America*, 138–39.

6. Donald Soper defines secularism as a "preoccupation with human affairs often to the exclusion of eternal well-being." Hunter writes that "'secularization' may be defined as 'the withdrawal of whole areas of life, thought, and activity from the control or influence of the church.'" George G. Hunter III, *How to Reach Secular People* (Nashville: Abingdon, 1992), 12, 25–26. For additional discussion of secularism, see his note on p. 173. I define *secularism* as the withdrawal of whole areas of life and thought from the control or influence of authentic, biblical Christianity.

7. James W. Sire, *The Universe Next Door: A Basic World View Catalog* (Downers Grove, Ill.: InterVarsity Press, 1976), 17.

8. Ibid., 18.

9. This is a topic often discussed in philosophy under the title *metaphysics*.

10. Ronald Nash writes that a well-rounded worldview touches five major areas: God, reality (metaphysics), knowledge (epistemolo-

219

Notes

gy), morality (ethics), and humankind. Ronald H. Nash, *World-Views in Conflict: Choosing Christianity in a World of Ideas* (Grand Rapids: Zondervan, 1992), 26.

11. This is not to say that other western worldviews do not exist. Because naturalism has proved to be a dead-end street, some have turned to nihilism and then, in response to nihilism, to existentialism and even New Age thought. Without question both nihilism, existentialism, and lately the New Age movement have affected American culture in the twentieth century. However, naturalism is the parent and more dominant worldview and the major competitor of Christianity. Therefore, in light of this and the fact that chapter 1 is not meant to be an extensive treatise on worldview, I have chosen to emphasize theism, deism, and naturalism.

12. Sire, *Universe Next Door*, 59.

13. Ibid., 73.

14. Francis Schaeffer, *How Should We Then Live?* (Old Tappen, N.J.: Fleming H. Revell, 1976), 39.

15. Kenneth Scott Latourette, *A History of Christianity* (New York: Harper and Row, 1953), 97.

16. Ibid., 513.

17. Schaeffer, *How Should We Then Live?*, 81.

18. Earle E. Cairns, *Christianity Through the Centuries* (Grand Rapids: Zondervan, 1954), 284.

19. Latourette, *History of Christianity*, 606.

20. Hunter, *Secular People*, 27.

21. Cairns, *Christianity*, 383–84.

22. Hunter, *Secular People*, 27.

23. Cairns, *Christianity*, 374.

24. Schaeffer, *How Shall We Then Live?*, 121.

25. Other elements of secularization also exist. For example, Hunter notes the major role that urbanization played in accelerating it. *See* Hunter, *Secular People*, 28–29.

26. Whereas the Enlightenment might be dated from 1689 to 1789, modern times or modernity is dated from 1789 to 1989 according to Thomas C. Oden, *Two Worlds* (Downers Grove, Ill.: InterVarsity Press, 1992), 32.

27. Martin Marty, *Righteous Empire: The Protestant Experience in America* (New York: Dial Press, 1970), 170.

28. Paul Johnson, *Modern Times: The World from the Twenties to the Nineties* (New York: Harper Perennial, 1992), 48.

29. Ibid.

30. Oden, *Two Worlds*, 37.

31. Latourette, *History of Christianity*, 1072.

32. Paul Johnson, *Modern Times*, 48.

33. Oden, *Two Worlds*, 33.

34. Ibid.

35. Ibid.

36. Ibid., 34.

37. Ibid., 35.

38. Ibid.

39. A fourth generation labeled the Echo Boom or the Baby Boomlet is coming along as well. They consist of approximately 50 million children who in 1993 are age eight and under. They will be knocking on the door of the church in the very late twentieth and early twenty-first centuries.

40. In fact, what follows serves only as a brief overview of each generation. Those who lead and minister in churches that desire high impact will need to study these generations in much greater detail. I would suggest that pastors start files on each group and read many of the books that have been written, especially recent works on the Baby Buster Generation.

41. Neil Howe and William Strauss, "The New Generation Gap," *Atlantic Monthly* 270, no. 6 (December 1992): 69.

42. Ibid., 72.

43. Ibid., 74, 81.

44. Ibid., 72.

45. Arthur J. De Jong, *Reclaiming a Mission* (Grand Rapids: Eerdmans, 1990), 12.

46. Ibid.

47. The years 1946–1964 are demographic figures. If viewed according to personality type, they represent those born between 1943 and 1960. "The New Generation Gap," *Atlantic Monthly*, (December 1992): 67.

48. Hans Finzel, *Help! I'm a Baby Boomer* (Wheaton: Victor Books, 1989), 16–17.

49. "President Clinton: Voters Show They Want a Change," *Dallas Morning News*, 4 November 1992.

50. Mary Ann Hogan, "Baby Boomers Getting Power," *Dallas Morning News*, 22 November 1992.

51. Finzel, *Baby Boomer,* 16, 86.

52. Mike Bellah, *Baby Boom Believers* (Wheaton: Tyndale House, 1988), 19.

53. Sydney E. Ahlstrom, *A Religious History of the American People* (New York: Yale University Press, 1972), 1087.

54. George Barna, "The Twenty-Something Crowd: Baby Busters," *Ministry Currents* (October–December 1992) 2, no. 4: 5.

55. Bill Marvel and Melissa Morrison, "The Pacifier People," *Dallas Morning News*, 7 February 1993.

56. Ibid.

57. Dieter Zander, "Baby Busters: How to Reach a New Generation," *The Pastor's Update* (November 1992): 6.

58. Marvel and Morrison, "Pacifier People."

59. Ibid.

60. Zander, "Baby Busters."

61. Marvel and Morrison, "Pacifier People."

62. De Jong, *Reclaiming a Mission*, 18.

63. Allan Bloom, *The Closing of the American Mind: Education and the Crisis of Reason* (New York: Simon and Schuster, 1987), 25.

Chapter 2: *The State of the American Church*

1. "The Weapons of War," *Leadership* (Spring 1993): 15.

2. Ibid.

3. De Jong, *Reclaiming a Mission*, 25–26.

4. Jackson W. Carroll, Douglas W. Johnson, and Martin E. Marty, *Religion in America: 1950 to the Present* (New York: Harper and Row, 1979), 41.

5. Ibid., 259.

6. George Gallup, Jr., *Religion in America—50 Years: 1935–1985*, (Princeton, N.J.: Gallup Report no. 236, 1985), 6.

7. Martin E. Marty, *Pilgrims in their Own Land: 500 Years of Religion in America* (Boston: Little, Brown and Company, 1984), 429–30.

8. Gallup, *Religion in America*, 7–8.

9. Ibid., 8.

10. Johnson, *Modern Times*, 4.

11. Gallup, *Religion in America*, 8.

12. Wade Clark Roof, "The Four Spiritual Styles of Baby Boomers," *USA Weekend*, 19–21 March 1993.

13. Gallup, *Religion in America*, 8.

14. Carroll, Johnson, and Marty, *Religion in America*, 41.

15. Ibid., 16.

16. De Jong, *Reclaiming a Mission*, 35.

17. George M. Marsden, "Are Secularists the Threat? Is Religion the Solution?" *Unsecular America,* ed. Richard John Neuhaus (Grand Rapids: Eerdmans, 1986), 37.

18. Thomas Ferguson and Joel Rogers, "The Myth of America's Turn to the Right," *Atlantic Monthly* 257 (May 1986): 43.

19. Mark Wingfield, "Diagnosis: 52 Percent of SBC Churches Stunted; 18 Percent on List of Critically Ill," *The Baptist Standard*, 12 December 1990, 12.

20. Tex Sample, *U.S. Lifestyles and Mainline Churches: A Key to Reaching People in the 90's* (Louisville: Westminster/John Knox Press, 1990), 5.

21. George Barna and William P. McKay, *Vital Signs: Emerging Social Trends and the Future of American Christianity* (Westchester, Ill.: Crossway, 1984), 4.

22. George Gallup, Jr., *The Unchurched American—10 Years Later* (Princeton, N.J.: Princeton Religion Research Center, 1988), 2.

23. Hunter, *Secular People*, 24.

24. C. Kirk Hadaway, Penny L. Marler, and Mark Chaves, "What the Polls Don't Show: A Closer Look at U.S. Church Attendance."

25. "Church Planting: A Bold New Approach to Evangelism in the 90s," *Ministry* (Summer 1991): 2.

26. Martin B. Bradley et al., *Churches and Church Membership in the United States 1990* (Atlanta: Glenmary Research Center, 1992), 1.

27. Jeffrey L. Sheler and Betsy Wagner, "Latter-day Struggles," *U.S. News and World Report*, 28 September 1992, 73.

28. Ibid., 74.

29. George Barna, *Today's Pastors* (Ventura, Calif.: Regal Books, 1993), 46.

30. Cheryl Heckler-Feltz, "Carter Attracts Lots of Visitors to Baptist Church in Plains," *Dallas Morning News*, 21 November 1992, religion section.

31. Laurie Wilson, "Bureau Predicts Population Surge," *Dallas Morning News*, 4 December 1992.

32. Ibid.

33. Roof, "Spiritual Styles," 5.

34. *National and International Religion Report*, 6 May 1991, 8.

35. Os Guinness, *The American Hour* (New York: The Free Press, 1993), 130.

36. Hunter, *Secular People*, 55.

37. Barna and McKay, *Vital Signs*, 136.

38. Michael Scott Horton, *Made in America: The Shaping of Modern American Evangelicalism* (Grand Rapids: Baker Book House, 1991), 33–34.

Chapter 3: *Hope for the Nation*

1. "Are We on the Verge of Revival?" *Charisma*, January 1993, 69–73.

2. Gallup, *Religion in America*, 14.

3. Ibid.

4. Ann Melvin, "Our Annual Search for More than Magic," *Dallas Morning News*, 5 December 1992.

5. Gallup, *Unchurched American*, 3.

6. Ibid.

7. Gallup, *Religion in America*, 14.

8. Ken Sidey, "A Generation on the Doorstep," *Moody Monthly*, January 1987, 23.

9. Jack Sims, "Baby Boomers: Time to Pass the Torch?" *Christian Life*, January 1986, 24.

10. Ibid.

11. Leith Anderson, *A Church for the 21st Century* (Minneapolis: Bethany House, 1992), 19.

12. Rolf Zettersten, "A Strategy for the Next Four Years," *Focus on the Family Magazine*, February 1993, 14.

13. Lance Morrow, "Man of the Year," *Time*, 4 January 1993, 24.

14. Oden, *Two Worlds*, 12.

15. Ibid., 32.

16. James B. Miller, "The Emerging Postmodern World," in *Postmodern Theology: Christian Faith in a Pluralist World*, ed. Frederic B. Burnham (San Francisco: Harper and Row, 1989), 7.

17. Millard J. Erickson, "A New Paradigm? Postmodernism and Hermeneutics" (Paper presented at the Forty-Third National Conference of The Evangelical Theological Society, Kansas City, Mo., 21–23 November 1991), 10–11.

18. Diogenes Allen, "Christian Values in a Post-Christian Context," in *Postmodern Theology*, ed. Burnham, 21.

19. Ibid., 23.

20. Ibid.

21. Ibid., 24.

22. Ibid.

23. Johnson, *Modern Times*, 1–5.

24. Harold K. Schilling, *The New Consciousness in Science and Religion* (Philadelphia: United Church Press, 1973), 44–45.

25. Allen, "Christian Values," 25.

26. Diogenes Allen, *Christian Belief in a Postmodern World* (Louisville: Westminster/John Knox Press, 1989), 2.

27. Oden, *Two Worlds*, 44–45.

28. Ibid., 55. *See also* Thomas C. Oden, "On Not Whoring After the Spirit of the Age," in *No God but God: Breaking with the Idols of Our Age*, eds. Os Guinness and John Seel (Chicago: Moody Press, 1992), 189–94.

29. James Davison Hunter, *American Evangelicalism: Conservative Religion and the Quandary of Modernity* (New Brunswick, N.J.: Rutgers University Press, 1983), 133.

Chapter 4: The Definition of a Vision

1. Kevin Maney, "IBM's Quest for Visionary," *USA Today*, 3 February 1993.

2. Diana Kunde, "What's Needed at IBM is Leader, not Manager," *Dallas Morning News*, 27 January 1993.

3. Lyle E. Schaller, *The Seven-Day-a-Week Church* (Nashville: Abingdon Press, 1992), 58, italics mine.

4. Robert Dale has written in the past on *vision* in his book *To Dream Again*

(Nashville: Broadman Press, 1981). Most recently I have addressed this topic in *Developing a Vision for Ministry in the 21st Century*, (Grand Rapids: Baker Book House, 1992) and George Barna has written *The Power of Vision* (Ventura, Calif.: Regal Books, 1992).

5. I deal with other vision relatives such as *dream*, *goals*, and *objectives* in *Developing a Vision for Ministry in the 21st Century*, 30–31.

6. In 1991, I conducted a survey of the faculty in the division of ministries at Dallas Theological Seminary. In this survey, I asked them to define a philosophy of ministry. The response revealed that most were defining it differently. Consequently, whenever I am in a discussion and the concept comes up, I always ask for a definition for purposes of clarity and accuracy.

7. Lyle E. Schaller, *Getting Things Done* (Nashville: Abingdon Press, 1986), 152–53.

8. For more information on the Meta-Church concept, *see* Carl George, *Prepare Your Church for the Future* (Grand Rapids: Fleming H. Revell, 1991).

9. Thomas S. Kuhn, *The Structure of Scientific Revolutions* (Chicago: University of Chicago Press, 1962).

10. De Jong, *Reclaiming a Mission*, 63.

11. Joel Arthur Barker, *Discovering the Future: The Business of Paradigms* (St. Paul: ILI Press, 1985), 14.

12. The concept of personal ministry vision is developed more fully in chaps. 5–6 of Aubrey Malphurs, *Planting Growing Churches for the Twenty-first Century* (Grand Rapids: Baker Book House, 1992). Chap. 5 explains the divine design concept in the context of personal ministry assessment. Chap. 6 takes the reader through the assessment process to help

him or her actually discover their personal ministry vision.

13. For an expanded discussion of this concept and how to develop a vision for one's ministry, *see* Malphurs, *Vision for Ministry*.

14. Chap. 5 in Malphurs, *Vision for Ministry*, discusses various creative ways for leaders to communicate their visions.

15. Malphurs, *Vision for Ministry*, 11.

16. John R. W. Stott, "What Makes Leadership Christian?" *Christianity Today*, August 1985, 24.

Chapter 5: *The Great Commission*

1. Malphurs, *Vision for Ministry*, 9.

2. In certain parts of the country, the community expected various professional people to be in church. For example, school boards and principals expected their teachers to be churched people.

3. The term *go* is a participle of attendant circumstance. As a general rule, it is translated as though its mood is the same as the finite verb which in verse 19 is the imperative "make disciples." Thus, it is an imperative and must be taken most seriously by the church. See Ernest De Witt Burton, *Syntax of the Moods and Tenses of New Testament Greek* (Edinburgh: T & T Clark, 1898), paragraphs 449–50.

4. Walter L. Liefeld, *Luke*, vol. 8 of *The Expositor's Bible Commentary*, ed. Frank E. Gabelein (Grand Rapids: Zondervan, 1984), 981.

5. Ibid., 1008.

6. Gallup, *Unchurched American*, 2.

7. Peter Wagner, "Church Growth Fine Tunes Its Formulas," *Christianity Today*, 24 June 1991, 46–47.

8. *Leadership Journal* (Spring 1992): 133; and Hunter, *Secular People*, 24.

9. Kennon Callahan, *Effective Church Leadership* (San Francisco: Harper and Row, 1990), 13.

10. Ibid., 8.

11. Ibid., 20.

12. Gallup, *Unchurched American*, 3.

13. Ibid., 4.

14. George Barna, "The Case of the Missing Boomers," *Ministry Currents* 2, no. 1 (January–March 1992): 2.

15. This would include such notables as CNN, *USA Today*, and *The Wall Street Journal*.

16. *Leadership Journal* (Spring 1992): 133.

17. Barna, "Missing Boomers," 2.

18. This concept is developed further in chapter 7.

19. Floyd Bartel, *A New Look at Church Growth* (Newton, Kans.: Faith and Life, 1987), 59.

20. George Barna, *The Frog in the Kettle* (Ventura, Calif.: Regal Books, 1990), 115.

21. Dan Griffiths, "Is the US Ready for DAWN?" *Dawn Report* (September 1992): 3; "Are We on the Verge of Revival?" *Charisma*, January 1993, 69.

22. Donald C. Posterski, *Reinventing Evangelism* (Downers Grove, Ill.: InterVarsity Press, 1989), 65.

23. Bill Hybels, *Honest to God?* (Grand Rapids: Zondervan, 1990), 126.

24. Ibid., 115–33.

25. Ibid., 127.

26. John R. W. Stott, *Our Guilty Silence* (Grand Rapids: Eerdmans, 1967), 13–16.

27. Posterski, *Reinventing Evangelism*, 15.

28. C. Peter Wagner, *Your Church Can Grow* (Ventura, Calif.: Regal Books, 1976), 111–12.

Chapter 6: *Planting Churches*

1. The purpose of this chapter is not to teach the reader how to plant churches. Those who are interested in planting churches should read Aubrey Malphurs, *Planting Growing Churches for the Twen-*

ty-first Century (Grand Rapids: Baker Book House, 1992).

2. For statistical purposes, the term *past* refers primarily to the decades from the Civil War up to World War I due to the lack of statistical information before this time.

3. Paulus Scharpff, *History of Evangelism* (Grand Rapids: Eerdmans, 1966), 312.

4. Lyle E. Schaller, *44 Questions for Church Planters* (Nashville: Abingdon Press, 1991), 15–20.

5. Ibid., 20.

6. Ibid., 16–17.

7. Ibid., 21.

8. Carroll, Johnson, and Marty, *Religion in America*, 41.

9. Win Arn, *The Pastor's Manual for Effective Ministry* (Monrovia, Calif.: Church Growth, 1988), 41, 43.

10. C. Peter Wagner, *Church Planting for a Greater Harvest* (Ventura, Calif.: Regal Books, 1990), 11.

11. Schaller, *44 Questions*, 23.

12. "The Phones for You" program was developed by Norm Whan in California. People in the core group call every household in the target community to invite them to church. The call is followed up by several letters and one last call to encourage those who have responded positively to follow through. For more information write Church Growth, Inc., 2670 South Myrtle Ave., Suite #201, Monrovia, CA 91016, or call (800) 423-4844.

13. Wagner, *Church Planting*, 38.

14. Callahan, *Church Leadership*, 260.

15. *See* Malphurs, *Planting Growing Churches*; chap. 3 for church planters who need help in fund-raising; chaps. 5–6 to assess a person's ability to lead a church-planting team.

16. Ibid., part 4, particularly chaps. 14, 16.

17. Ibid., 67–68.

18. Some might argue that this approach discourages the development of talented people within the planted church. Experience indicates that this is not the case. Generally, people who are truly talented and gifted in an area are attracted to quality. Those who are not are encouraged to discover their true areas of giftedness.

19. *See* Malphurs, *Planting Growing Churches*, 248–55.

20. Lyle E. Schaller, "Southern Baptists Face Two Choices for Future," *Biblical Recorder*, 27 April 1991, 8.

21. I add the term *organizational* because some who might be thought of as a denomination view that as negative and prefer to be seen otherwise.

22. Barna, *Frog in the Kettle*, 141.

23. Wagner, *Church Planting*, 12.

24. "U.S. Religion in Transition," *Dallas Morning News*, 13 March 1990.

25. Les Parrott III and Robin D. Perrin, "The New Denominations," *Christianity Today*, 11 March 1991, 29.

26. *National and International Religion Report*, 6 May 1991, 2.

27. Ibid.

28. Larry Lewis, "The 15,000 Campaign," *Missions USA* (July–August 1991): 34.

29. Parrott and Perrin, "New Denominations," 30.

30. Various figures are available. Richard Ostling cites 429 churches in *Time*, 5 April 1993, 47. Parrott and Perrin give 356 domestic and 350 international for a total of 706 churches in *Christianity Today*, 11 March 1991, 31. I have an undated list of affiliate churches in America that totals more than 400.

31. Parrott and Perrin, "New Denominations," 30.

32. Leith Anderson, speaking to Advanced Church Planting class, Dallas Theological Seminary, 23 March 1993.

33. Hunter, *Secular People,* 153.

34. Stan Guthrie, "Best Missions Churches Share Their Trade Secrets," *World Pulse,* 12 March 1993, 1.

35. Hunter, *Secular People,* 153.

Chapter 7: Renewing Churches

1. The purpose of this chapter is not to cover how a church accomplishes revitalization. Those who are interested in the renewal process should read Aubrey Malphurs, *Pouring New Wine into Old Wineskins* (Grand Rapids: Baker Book House, 1993).

2. American folklore tells the story of a young boy who lived in a town that was occasionally endangered by wolves. Whenever a person was threatened by a wolf, that person would yell "wolf," and all the town's people would come running to help. One boy yelled "wolf" when there was no wolf, simply for the fun of seeing all the people stop what they were doing and come running to help. Of course, one day a wolf did come, and the boy cried "wolf," but no one responded. The moral of this story is obvious.

3. Leith Anderson, *A Church for the 21st Century* (Minneapolis: Bethany House, 1992), 41.

4. Michael E. Gerber, *The E-Myth* (New York: Harper Business, 1986), 156.

5. Pat Baldwin, "Forecasting the '90s," *Dallas Morning News,* 27 October 1991.

6. Alvin Toffler, *Power Shift* (New York: Bantam Books, 1990), 228.

7. Ibid., xvii.

8. Joel Arthur Barker, *Discovering the Future* (St. Paul: ILI Press, 1985), 2–3.

9. C. Kirk Hadaway, *Church Growth Principles* (Nashville: Broadman Press, 1991), 110.

10. Lyle E. Schaller, *Strategies for Change* (Nashville: Abingdon Press, 1993), 40.

11. For example, see the chart on denominations and movements in Parrott and Perrin, "New Denominations," 29.

12. Callahan, *Church Leadership,* 26.

13. Ralph Neighbour, Jr., *Where Do We Go from Here?* (Houston: Touch Publications, 1990), 92.

14. Lyle E. Schaller, *The Change Agent* (Nashville: Abingdon Press, 1972), 11.

15. George Barna, *User Friendly Churches* (Ventura, Calif.: Regal Books, 1991), 22.

16. Schaller, *Strategies for Change,* 10, italics mine.

17. Callahan, *Church Leadership,* 4.

18. C. Peter Wagner, *Your Church Can Grow* (Ventura, Calif.: Regal Books, 1976), 61.

19. Lyle E. Schaller, *Activating the Passive Church* (Nashville: Abingdon Press, 1981), 11.

20. *See* Malphurs, *Pouring New Wine,* chaps. 3–4, for an extended development of this important biblical concept.

21. These two profiles are the same. The difference is that the latter explains the different temperaments in light of Bible characters. They can be ordered from the Charles E. Fuller Institute of Evangelism and Church Growth, P. O. Box 91990, Pasadena, CA 91109-1990, telephone: (800) 999-9578.

22. John G. Geier and Dorothy E. Downey, *Personal Profile System* (Minneapolis: Performax Systems International, 1977), 17.

23. For an expanded discussion of temperament and renewal using various personality tools, see Malphurs, *Pouring New Wine,* 64–70.

24. Barker, *Discovering the Future,* 35.

25. Ibid., 25.

26. Ibid., 37.

27. Gary Friesen, *Decision Making and the Will of God* (Portland, Oreg.: Multnomah Press, 1980).

28. See the further development of this concept in chap. 4.

29. Schaller, *Strategies for Change*, 86.

30. However, this is not always the case. Some seminary graduates have virtually no courses in leadership or church-based experience in the same. Certain astute lay board members quickly discern this and take over the reigns of leadership before disaster strikes. Also, leading voluntary organizations is sufficiently different from leading nonvoluntary organizations that Peter Drucker has addressed the differences in *Managing the Nonprofit Organization* (New York: HarperCollins, 1990) and *The Changing World of the Executive* (New York: Times Books, 1982), chaps. 18–24.

31. Schaller, *Strategies for Change*, 86.

32. *See* an insightful discussion of this idea in Peter Wagner, *Leading Your Church to Growth* (Ventura, Calif.: Regal Books, 1984), 119–20.

33. Lyle E. Schaller, *Growing Plans* (Nashville: Abingdon Press, 1983), 85.

34. Lyle E. Schaller, *Create Your Own Future!* (Nashville: Abingdon Press, 1991), 22.

35. *See* Malphurs, *Planting Growing Churches*, chap. 8, for a theology of church leadership.

36. Schaller, *Growing Plans*, 48.

37. Gary L. McIntosh, *The McIntosh Church Growth Network* 2, No. 6 (June 1990). To receive the McIntosh reports, write to *The McIntosh Church Growth Network*, 3630 Camellia Drive, San Bernardino, CA 92404.

38. Elaine Dickson, *Say No, Say Yes to Change* (Nashville: Broadman Press, 1982), 84.

39. For other reasons why people resist change and for some ways to handle these situations, *see* Malphurs, *Pouring New Wine*, chap. 5.

40. *Great Commission Breakthrough Consultant's Manual* (Nashville: Convention Press, 1992), 8.

41. James E. Thuirer, "Catching the Spirit of Vision 2000 Evangelism," *Discipleship Dateline*, May 1993, 3.

42. Frank R. Tillapaugh, *Unleashing the Church* (Ventura, Calif.: Regal Books, 1982), 6.

43. This concept has been developed by Carl George, director of the Fuller Institute of Evangelism and Church Growth. He explains the concept in *Prepare Your Church for the Future*.

Chapter 8: Renewing Theological Education

1. A system based in the private sector, its training takes place on the job. The typical apprentice spends four days a week at his training company and one day in a public vocational school for two to three years in any of 380 occupations.

2. Some well-known examples are the pastors conferences held at Grace Community Church (John McArthur), Saddleback Valley Community Church (Rick Warren), and Willow Creek Community Church (Bill Hybels).

3. BILD, International (Biblical Institute of Leadership Development) is an organization championed by Mr. Jeff Reed, Dr. Gene Getz, and Dr. Ted Ward to promote church-based theological education.

4. A Conservative Baptist Association school begun in 1985 with classes that meet only one day per week. It is located in north suburban Philadelphia, Pennsylvania, in Worcester, Massachusetts, and the New York Center holds classes in Manhattan.

Notes

5. Established in 1983 in the Chesapeake region of Virginia, its enrollment has expanded to nearly 140 part-time students who meet at night in churches throughout Virginia, Maryland, and Delaware.

6. A matter that I discussed earlier in chapter 6.

7. H. Richard Niebuhr, *The Purpose of the Church and Its Ministry: Reflections on the Aims of Theological Education* (New York: Harper and Brothers, 1956), 107.

8. R. Paul Stevens, "Marketing the Faith—A Reflection on the Importing and Exporting of Western Theological Education," *Crux*, June 1992, 9.

9. Ibid.

10. Ibid.

11. Anderson, *21st Century*, 47.

12. Ibid.

13. Lyle E. Schaller, "Megachurch!" *Christianity Today*, 5 March 1990, 23.

14. Stevens, "Marketing the Faith," 9.

15. Yet many institutions fail to adequately compensate their faculties, allotting finances, instead, for buildings, promotions, and other matters.

16. Stevens, "Marketing the Faith," 15.

17. George Brushaber, "The Twenty-first Century Seminary," *Christianity Today*, 17 May 1993, 46.

18. Stevens, "Marketing the Faith," 9.

19. Anderson, *21st Century*, 74.

20. *See* Hunter, *Secular People*.

21. Schaller, *Getting Things Done*, 146.

22. Robert Altmeyer, "Education in the Arts and Sciences: Divergent Paths" (Ph.D. diss., Carnegie Institute of Technology, 1966) quoted in Jay A. Conger, *The Charismatic Leader* (San Francisco: Jossey-Bass, 1989), 163.

23. Bruce L. Shelley, "The Seminaries' Identity Crisis," *Christianity Today*, 17 May 1993, 42.

24. This does not mean to imply that the exegesis of Scripture or thinking theologically are not important. In fact, they are vital and at the core of any pastoral ministry. Those who lead God's church in any era must be able to exegete Scripture and think theologically.

25. Shelley, "Identity Crisis," 42.

26. Anderson, *21st Century*, 75–76.

27. James M. Kouzes and Barry Z. Posner, *The Leadership Challenge* (San Francisco: Jossey-Bass, 1987), 284.

28. Stevens, "Marketing the Faith," 18.

29. A more accurate term than *pedagogy* is *androgogy*, the art of teaching adults.

30. Stevens, "Marketing the Faith," 10.

31. Ibid., 12.

32. Brushaber, "Twenty-First Century Seminary," 46.

33. Ibid.

34. For more details see Daniel Cattau, "Some Fear Baptist College Trading Values for Success," *Dallas Morning News*, 16 May 1993.

35. Schaller, "Megachurch!" 23.

36. Ibid.

37. Stevens, "Marketing the Faith," 12.

Index

Index

Aubrey Malphurs is the president of Vision Ministries International and is available for consultation on various topics related to leadership, vision, church planting, church renewal, etc. Those wishing to contact him for consulting or speaking engagements may do so through the following:

Vision Ministries International
5041 Urban Crest
Dallas, TX 75227
1-214-841-3777